SLUMS REIMAGINED

How Informal Settlements Help the Poor Overcome Poverty and Model
Sustainable Neighborhoods for All

Aaron Smith

Urban Loft Publishers | Skyforest, CA

Slums Reimagined

How Informal Settlements Help the Poor Overcome Poverty and Model Sustainable Neighborhoods for All

Urban Loft Publishers
P.O. Box 6
Skyforest, CA 92385
www.urbanloftpublishers.com

Senior Editors: Stephen Burris & Kendi Howells Douglas
Copy Editor: Marla Black
Graphics: Brittnay Parsons
Cover Design: Elizabeth Arnold

ISBN-13: 978-1-949-625-07-3

Made in the U.S

Praise for *Slums Reimagined*

Aaron Smith presents an eye-opening, alternative approach to addressing the critical challenges in poverty and housing. His decades of experience in informal settlements has produced practical insights for any agency combatting homelessness.

> -Marisa Lin, Program Performance Auditor, City of San Jose

Slums Reimagined is a paradigm shift especially to those who have stereotyped the slums as a problem in the society. Dr. Aaron smith writes from his heart as he experienced firsthand the beauty of the slum community! As a community organizer of such community, I too can attest to his insights. Slums have much to offer than we think. This is indeed a good read!

> -Edna Andaya Te, Community Organizer in a large informal settlement, Quezon City

Aaron Smith is in a unique position to help us understand this positive and intriguing perspective on informal communities – or slums as most of the minority world would name them. Growing up in America, Aaron came to live in an informal community in Manila, Philippines as a young adult. He fell in love, married and is now raising a family, living long-term in a community which he convincingly argues is a healthier and safer place to live than most of his readers can imagine. I have visited Aaron's home and neighborhood and have seen the reality of the positive social connections. Because of his multicultural perspective, Aaron is able to relate his life learning to American and other contexts, generalizing the applications to other cities with possibilities of enabling the poor to overcome poverty and creating truly sustainable neighborhoods.

> -Dr Irene Alexander, Lecturer in Manila, Philippines and Brisbane Australia, and Elder for Servants to Asia's Urban Poor

There are few urban leaders who have so internalized what justice looks like for modern cities that their ideas for transformation reach into the realm of the radical and revolutionary. Aaron Smith is one of them. His decades of urban transformation experience and scholarship have given him keen insight into what radical justice and poverty alleviation practically looks like for marginalized urban poor communities. This book will challenge you to radically reimagine how to view slum communities, as well as the systemic policies and practices that lead to their flourishing.

> -Alex Dobbs, Urban Youth Worker and Community Organizer, East Los Angeles

Slums Reimagined is a book that is critical for all city councilors and city planners to read, if not for all people in general. It shatters all stereotypes of what people think of when they hear the word "slum," because it beautifully describes the assets, strengths and gifts that we need more of in this world, especially in the West where our sense of community has been so fragmented. Smith shares from his personal first-hand experiences of living in the slum community of Botocan for the past decade. He reminds us that we have so much to learn from resilient and creative urban poor people, and how they have much knowledge to offer the world about how they have learned to survive and thrive. On a personal and macro level, the world could learn and implement important changes in how to support and improve urban poor communities directly from those who know best how to do that--the urban poor themselves, and how they have supported and advocated for themselves. This book is the next best thing to seeing a slum community through an accurate lens for yourself in person.

-Sharon Song, Spiritual Director, Urban Minister in South Los Angeles

I had the pleasure of visiting Botocan, the neighborhood in which Aaron lives. I remember the smile on one resident's face as he recounts the early stages of rebuilding of his home after a devastating fire. The roof had not yet been put on during his first night's sleep, but he was ecstatic because he could "see the stars." We oftentimes forget that life-moments are not experienced in a vacuum or in outer space, but in a specific place: the day you hear back from a job interview, the first time you hold hands with a loved one, a time you saw the stars. In the following pages, Aaron gives us an invitation to imagine the significance of place for the world's most vulnerable. If you dare to accept the invitation, you will learn to see the world and the people in it; it will challenge you not to ignore the pains of poverty in order to find a fleetingly romantic silver lining, but to examine an opportunity for a joy that comes from having enough.

-Derrick Sanderlin, Community Organizer and Creative in San Jose, CA

This book is dedicated to the world's informal settlers,
who are building sustainable and livable communities against
overwhelming odds.

Table of Contents

Foreword

I visited Botocan in the summer of 2013 as part of an internship with Servant Partners, an organization that partners with indigenous community leaders toward transformative change. Aaron was not only one of my hosts in the community, but an essential guide to contextualizing my time there.

Just three months prior I had completed an undergraduate degree in urban studies from the University of California, Irvine; this was not only a canonical study on city design and operation, but a study that took place in the peculiar context of Irvine, California. Since its inception as a master plan city, Irvine has not overlooked any detail of its existence. Each neighborhood has predetermined architectural standards to give it a distinct character; each street is lined with a carefully curated arboreal collection. Irvine is exquisitely crafted suburbia, an unambiguous maximization of the American dream.

My first few steps into Botocan quickly forced me to reckon with a new paradigm of community. I can remember gazing out across the city from the roof of a concrete house, marveling at the chaotic assembly of power lines, the layered corrugated roofs, the bustle of the basketball court. I sat on the roof for at least an hour trying to take in every detail of a variegated scene. I thought Botocan could not be more opposite from Irvine in its construction, organization, regulation, and design.

These two paradigms - Botocan and Irvine, the slum and the suburb - are imaginations. They are radically different visions through which communities leverage economy and space, the environments in which we live our lives and view our world. To be unaware of our communal imagination is to delude ourselves, and to the extent that we are delusional, it could be said that we are *imagining things*. That is, if we are unaware of the paradigm that frames our communities, we may begin to materialize the objects of our communal aspirations without ever having considered critically their materialization.

As a resident of two paradigms, Aaron incisively peels away the objects of our delusion: lawns, low densities, cars, zoning restrictions... These are not new problems for the American city planner or architect who acknowledge the absurdities; neither is it new to reimagine remedies. But Aaron is calling for a deeper reimagination, one without an ingrained injustice towards the poor. To read this book as an exhaustive list of planning or design solutions, or to read it only as a list of problems with the suburban paradigm would be to reduce this text to an object of our current imagination - another book dissatisfied with the suburban project. Aaron doesn't only ask us to rethink the objects of our delusion - our neighborhoods themselves - but also to take stock of the nature of our reimaginations. He asks us to think about our neighborhoods more as means than ends: means to economic security, means to social connection, means to sustainable living. If people - but especially the poor - are not at the fore of our new imagination, then surely we are playing out old imaginations with new things.

This book comes at another critical moment in my life as I begin a career in architecture. I can't help but remember my time in Botocan, and the impact it had in shaping my imagination of what a neighborhood could be. Aaron's ability to tease out the ethical underpinnings of his environment and contextualize them with authority could not be more timely or more needed. I'm confident his words will continue to shape my speculations, my hopes, and my reimagination for the neighborhoods around me.

Kevin MacDougall
Los Angeles, California

Preface

Do slums help or hurt the poor? This question cannot be answered generically, because the answer depends on the specific slum in question. Many slums crush and oppress the poor, but this does not have to be the case. My experience is that under the right conditions, slums can help the residents improve their lives and overcome poverty.

This book examines the conditions needed for communities to help the poor overcome poverty. It looks at how the poor themselves build communities to meet their needs and why these communities can serve as a model for sustainable neighborhoods. The thesis of this book is that those living in poverty know how to build neighborhoods that meet their needs and have much to offer on how to help the poor overcome poverty. In order to defend this thesis, neighborhood design is examined from the perspective of those living in poverty.

I have lived in informal settlements for almost my entire adult life. Through this experience I slowly learned how informal settlements help the poor improve their lives. The years have been filled with joys and pains. Life is not easy in an informal settlement, but suffering is not the only experience. There is also great joy as the community develops and peoples' lives improve.

I am fully aware of poverty's devastating effects. This is in no way an attempt to romanticize poverty. Nor am I fatalistically cursing the poor to a lifetime of poverty. This book is the exact opposite. It provides hope for the poor by looking at their own resources and ingenuity.

The idea that there are positive features of informal settlements can be threatening. Perhaps even more controversial is my claim that incorporating these neighborhood features in the design of communities can reduce urban poverty.

I am certainly not the first person to recognize that informal settlements have much to offer. The residents themselves often have a much higher view of their community than wealthier outsiders. Even so, the good within informal settlements has not escaped notice. Journalist and investigative reporter Robert Neuwirth developed a positive view of informal settlements after spending a few months living in four different ones on four different continents. He writes,

> The true challenge is not to eradicate these communities but to stop treating them as slums-that is, as horrific, scary, and criminal-and start treating them as neighborhoods that can be improved. They don't need to be knocked down and built new, because in most cases this will only produce housing that is not affordable to the people who are living there.[1]

Urbanist Sean Benesh writes of informal settlements, "Rather than viewing these areas as problems, we instead need to see them as hotbeds for innovation."[2] The poor living in informal settlements are not passively wallowing in their poverty. They are responding in creative ways to improve their lives when they are not punished for doing so.

A well-known voice speaking favorably of informal settlements is England's Prince Charles. He mentioned their positive features in a speech after visiting Mumbai. During this speech, Prince Charles said:

> I find an underlying, intuitive "grammar of design" – that subconsciously produces somewhere that is walkable, mixed-use and adapted to local climate and materials, which is totally absent from the faceless slab blocks that are still being built around the world to "warehouse" the poor, despite their failure

here in Britain and, indeed, in other highly developed economies in past decades.[3]

Prince Charles recognized that informal settlements are walkable, mixed-use, and built with locally available materials that are suited for that location. He also acknowledged that the community the poor built themselves better meets their needs than the ones that governments build for them. These are all easily observable characteristics of many informal settlements.

I too had quickly recognized some of the positive aspects of informal settlements. However, it took years to fully comprehend just how informal settlements help the poor overcome poverty. People are getting out of poverty not in spite of the informal settlement they live in but because of it.

Two back-to-back events in my life helped me to see the positive aspects of informal settlements. The first was the demolition of the informal settlement along the railroad tracks in Manila. I had lived in that community for about seven years when the demolition notice came. The residents were angry about the destruction of their community and tried to stop the demolition. If informal settlements are so bad, why do the residents not welcome demolition? If their goal in life is to move out, why is it that when governments make them move they do not cheer and celebrate?

Across the globe, whenever a government attempts to bulldoze an informal settlement or tent city the residents fight to save their homes. Everywhere from the railroad community in Manila, to the highest informal settlement, the Tower of David in Venezuela, to the Jungle, one of the largest informal settlements in the US, all protested the destruction of their community. There is no denying the fact that at least for the residents, informal settlements offer something worth fighting for.

The other event that made me reflect on the positive aspects of informal settlements was after I moved to Botocan, in Quezon City, Philippines. At first I was frustrated with myself because I could not determine what the residents felt were their community's biggest problems. I was still seeing informal settlements as I was conditioned to, as places full of problems to be solved. I struggled to determine the community's problems because everyone I talked to seemed to focus on why Botocan was a great place to live. The response I was getting from the residents was "we're squatters but we're different, we're orderly and good." They have also been socially conditioned to view informal settlements as problems. Yet, they also know that their neighborhood does not fit the negative stereotype of informal settlements. One of the striking features of Botocan is the perception by the residents that their community is unique in a good way. It took a while for me to finally accept that the people really liked their community.

Botocan will serve as the main case study throughout this book. The pain and suffering because of poverty and oppression is already well documented, so I will not deal with that side of living in informal settlements. I am intentionally focusing on the positive features of the community in order to show that it was built around the needs of the residents and helps them overcome poverty.

This book is not full of rags to riches stories. That is not what overcoming poverty means for most people. A family overcoming poverty means they eat three meals a day and are able to pay their monthly bills. Many would still consider them poor, but they have stability in their lives.

Policy makers, city planners, architects, and society as a whole need a paradigm shift regarding how slums are viewed. This book is a call to intentionally build communities that help the poor overcome poverty by integrating the wisdom of the poor into neighborhood design. It is no longer acceptable to force the poor to live in oppressive neighborhoods that hinder their efforts to improve their lives.

Part I

Seeing Beyond Shanties

I first moved into an informal settlement in Manila soon after graduating from college. My home was just a few feet from active railroad tracks. Life there was difficult, very difficult. Yet after a while, I began to realize that the residents liked their neighborhood and were happy there. They did not want to move.

At first, I thought they liked their community because slum life was all they knew. They did not know what a nice neighborhood was like and therefore they were content to stay in their community. Slowly I began to realize that this was not the case at all. While the middle and upper classes are ignorant about how the poor live, those in poverty know all too well the lifestyle of the upper classes. This is because popular media portrays luxurious living as normal.

I also began to realize that the suburban community where I had grown up was not as ideal as I was socially conditioned to believe. Communities that foster life are not necessarily the most expensive or exclusive. Could it be that the neighborhoods offering the most to their residents are informal settlements? The amazing features of informal settlements are not obvious at first glance, but for those who take the time to look beyond the squalor and grime, a new image begins to emerge. When we look closely, the ingenuity and practicality of the design of informal settlements becomes apparent. The seemingly horrendous appearances of informal settlements with homes constructed of secondhand materials are safer and more livable than most outside observers think.

1

Prejudice Against Slums

Before becoming open to the idea that informal settlements help the poor overcome poverty and have something positive to offer the world, it is important to reevaluate the images we have in our mind when we think of these neighborhoods. Some of the reactions to informal settlements are so far from reality they are almost comical. I saw a video of tourists in Manila that showed them driving next to an informal settlement. The brief clip of wooden shanties and the community's residents is interrupted when a passenger panics because they were too close to the community. The video ends with someone yelling, "Put the window up!" It is really quite sad that small piecework homes and poor people are considered so scary that getting too close to them is terrifying.

Prejudice against slums and the poor is fairly universal. In the suburban town where I grew up, there was a low-income neighborhood with modest sized row homes. I remember being told, "Don't drive through that neighborhood unless you're going 55 mph with the windows up." This statement echoes the same assumption as the tourists in Manila. Slums are so dangerous that being in a moving vehicle is not enough protection.

Slumophobia

Out of pain and struggle, informal settlements emerge as the poor's solution to their own problems. Yet, because they exist on the margins of society, these communities are often misunderstood. They are labeled as slums and treated like they are the scariest places on earth. This fear is what I call slumophobia.

There are well-educated, intelligent people that have an irrational fear of slums. They are convinced that they will be victimized if they go near a slum. The conventional wisdom that all slums are dangerous is based on a limited set of facts that do not tell the whole story. Not all slums are dangerous and not everyone who lives in a slum is a criminal.

Are All Slums Dangerous?

A neighborhood with low-income residents does not automatically make it dangerous. Yet, the common assumption is that all slums are dangerous. People who have never lived in a slum have told me, "You better not walk through that neighborhood without body armor." And, "Don't go there, they will rob you down to your underwear." The app Ghetto Tracker renamed Good Part of Town was developed to help people avoid neighborhoods deemed to be unsafe.4 It is as if slums need to be avoided like the plague.

The social conditioning to view all low-income communities as dangerous is so strong that even the poor can be afraid of unfamiliar slums. I learned this lesson after a friend from another informal settlement visited me. He lived his entire life in one of the most notorious slums in Manila. After our visit, I walked him out of my community. Once we entered the neighboring middle-class community, he patted himself down and said that he was thankful to get out alive. Confused, I asked him what he was afraid of, and he responded that there were some scary people in my neighborhood. I told him the people here were scared of those from his community.

Some slums are dangerous, and there are crime rates to prove it. However, just because one specific slum has a high murder rate does not mean that every low-income community on the planet does. The murder rate of a neighborhood is never used to define a slum. Yes, of course it is unwise to walk around unescorted by a local resident in certain communities. No, I will not walk around a random slum in the middle of the night. No matter what neighborhood you are in, basic streetwise caution is always advised. I am not arguing that informal settlements are crime free utopias. What I am saying is that there are other stories coming from these communities and when we only focus on violence we miss the beauty.

Informal settlements are communities where people live. Most informal settlements are not as dangerous as they are imagined to be. "The stereotypes of poor communities are often scarier than the actual realities of day-to-day life."[5] Violence in informal settlements is usually connected to domestic problems, drugs, or police instigated. Random violence is rare and does not plague all or even most informal settlements. Yet, slumophobia still persists.

The reality is that not all informal settlements are dangerous. In fact, they can be safer than the city in which they are located. I am much more likely to be robbed, mugged, or assaulted whenever I leave Botocan, the informal settlement where I currently live, than I am within my neighborhood.

The violence that is prevalent in some slums, particularly in the US is directly connected to failed community design, and oppressive policies. The poor are not inherently violent and not all slums have to be feared.

Are Slums Full of Criminals?

Conventional wisdom has pounded it in our heads that criminals live in slums. The residents of low-income communities are certainly more likely to be arrested and convicted of a crime, but this says more about unjust policing and an oppressive criminal justice system than it does about the relationship between poverty and criminality. A rich teenager living in a gated subdivision can drive around with drugs in her luxury car and never even think of the possibility of being stopped by the police. A teenager walking home from school in a low-income community doing nothing wrong can be stopped by the police and arrested without cause. Without knowledge of the law or the ability to afford a lawyer, the teen is powerless to challenge the police. According to the numbers, the rich kid is law abiding while the teen from a slum is a criminal. Reality is much more complicated.

The perception that the poor are all criminals is simply not true. Slums do not have nearly as many hoodlums waiting to rob and kill as we are led to believe. Low-income communities certainly have their share of criminals, but the vast majority of community residents are law abiding. One of my neighbors found the latest model iPhone that someone dropped. He immediately went to the contacts and called the owner's mom to inform her about the lost phone. Within an hour, the owner came to claim her lost phone. My neighbor knew exactly how much money he could have sold the iPhone for, yet he returned it without hesitation.

Crimes that occur in wealthy neighborhoods are often blamed on the poor. It is simply assumed that thieves do not live in "nice" communities. I spoke with a resident of a suburb 30 miles outside of Washington DC who blamed a recent break-in on someone from the housing projects in DC. This scenario is repeated over and over whenever there is a property crime; the poor are the first suspects.

The criminality in low-income communities is also because unjust laws criminalize efforts to overcome poverty. When someone who lives in America's slums tries to buy legal products cheap and resell them from their home they are charged with zoning violations and risk fines, evictions, and even jail. In the case of Eric Garner you get execution by strangulation. When the poor take action to try to improve their lives they are punished by social services and the American criminal justice system.

Reinforcing Negative Stereotypes

Many of the prejudices against slums come from the way they are misrepresented in the media. If all I knew about slums came from popular media, I would also be slumophobic. Popular media takes specific issues facing slum residents and magnifies them to the point of creating tunnel vision. Yes, there are shootings in some slums, but not every minute of every day. Neighborhoods that go a significant amount of time without gunshots do not make exciting news reports.

The media often overemphasizes drugs and violence in slums. I have seen news reports in low-income communities where the reporter walked around in body armor while being accompanied by a police officer. This created the image that simply being in an impoverished neighborhood put the reporter in so much danger of being shot that they needed body armor and a police escort. This sensationalism is more entertainment than actual journalism.

The movie industry cannot resist cashing in on the hype of violent slums. Movies set in slums make shootouts look like an everyday occurrence. Yes, violence does happen in inner cities, and it is important for the middle class to know about it. I have witnessed urban violence firsthand when I was caught in the crossfire of a shootout. I have no desire to minimize the violence that does happen, but it is also important to be realistic. The image of extreme violence with constant gunfire is grossly exaggerated. Nor does it take into account that someone is more likely to die in a car accident than by random violence in a low-income community, but that does not sell movie tickets.

Even governments join the fight to get the public to hate slums. Slums were the target of an aggressive public opinion advertising campaign designed to make the average American want their removal. In 1936, the New York City Housing Authority released a poster stating, "Eliminate crime in the slums through housing." Another poster released the same year read: "Cure juvenile delinquency in the slums by planned housing." The United States Housing Authority made advertisement posters to convince the public that slums made criminals with a poster from 1941 that read "Slums Breed Crime." That same year they released a poster demanding "Cross Out Slums."

The news, movies, and government all have an agenda to make slums look like bad places to live. There is certainly much to improve about slums, which will be briefly examined in chapter 12. The point is that the complete picture of slums is not shown. There are other aspects to these communities besides drugs and violence. Over 1.4 billion people call slums home, and some of them have made it a safe, happy, and admirable place to live.

Emphasizing the Negative

Slums are often viewed as places full of problems. The term slum itself is negative, and I only use it in an effort to help reframe the way we think about these communities. The overwhelming emphasis is on negative characteristics. Some of the common ways slums are characterized are substandard housing, run-down, dirty, grungy, unsanitary, and unfit for human habitation.

The UN-Habitat classifies slums under two broad categories, slums of hope and slums of despair.[6] Categorizing a community as a slum of despair is about as negative as you can get. It sounds like the name of a horror movie. I can imagine the opening scene with scary music in the background, and a creepy voice saying, "slum of despair" followed by screams. It gives me goose bumps just thinking about it. For the fantasy world of horror movies that's fine. But when you are talking about where real people live it is degrading and offensive.

The UN-Habitat defines slums by focusing on their deficiencies.

A slum household consists of one or a group of individuals living under the same roof in an urban area, lacking one or more of the following five amenities: (1) durable housing (a permanent structure providing protection from extreme climatic conditions); (2) sufficient living area (no more than three people sharing a room); (3) access to improved water (water that is sufficient, affordable and can be obtained without extreme effort); (4) access to improved sanitation facilities (a private toilet, or a public one shared with a reasonable number of people); and (5) secure tenure (*de facto* or *de jure* secure tenure status and protection against forced evictions).[7]

The UN-Habitat definition recognizes valid issues of urban poverty that need to be addressed. Structurally sound housing, access to water, adequate sanitation, and land security are important aspects of communities that help the poor improve their lives. Of course other issues could have been included such as access to education, health care, and employment.

The UN-Habitat definition is very convenient for governments because it focuses on issues that have specific solutions and are measurable. Projects simply have to address one of the five areas that slums lack and you have a successful project.

Defining slums this way is unfair and insults the residents of these communities. It is very hard to see the beauty of a community when it is defined by its deficiencies. This is one reason why some people are so against the idea that informal settlements help the poor improve their lives.

Defining communities by their problems can also be done for wealthy neighborhoods. I spent an afternoon in Los Angeles' premier city, Beverly Hills.[8] We parked next to a Lamborghini and walked passed a Ferrari, just to give an example of the amount of money there. Yet, I can still define Beverly Hills by what it lacks.

Beverly Hills contains households that lack one or more of the following:

1. Meaningful relationships with neighbors.
2. Safety in the event of a freak accident inside the home. (No one has a clue if a neighbor has a heart attack or is in any kind of trouble.)
3. Safe hangout spots within biking distance for youth.
4. Stores within walking distance to buy basic goods. (This lack contributes to traffic, increased carbon emissions, and the risk of traffic related injuries.)

5.   Security of investment in the event that new housing trends cause multimillion-dollar homes to become unsellable.

Living in a multimillion-dollar home in Beverly Hills does not seem nearly as appealing when it is defined by what it lacks. Of course, this is an entirely unfair and one-sided description of Beverly Hills. That's the point. Defining slums purely by what they lack or by what is wrong with them is an injustice to the poor who call those places home.

Defining slums by their problems creates the mindset that they need to be fixed. This is seen in the calls for the elimination of slums. Cities Without Slums is a global movement organized by Cities Alliance in partnership with the World Bank and UN-Habitat. Their goals reflect the desire to truly help people living in poverty. Yet the name reflects a very negative view of slums.

The seemingly honorable goal to have cities without slums, simply assumes that society would be better off without slums. The focus on the elimination of slums can result in further impoverishing the poor as they are forced to move to oppressive neighborhoods. Instead of cities without slums, the goal should be cities without injustice, oppression, and poverty. The reality is that all urban residents regardless of social class would lose a beautiful aspect of urban living if low-income communities are simply eliminated and replaced with middle-class housing. In the effort to improve the quality of life of all urban residents we must avoid throwing the baby out with the bathwater with the loss of the positive features of informal settlements.[9]

Slums Make Us Uncomfortable

Perhaps the biggest reason slums receive such negative reaction is because they make us feel uncomfortable. They nag at our conscience. Slums display for all to see how society has failed its most vulnerable citizens.

Instead of changing unjust laws, the response has been to change the slums. Programs are started to rescue the poor from slums. Slum upgrade projects supposedly make low-income communities more livable, but in reality most simply make them look nicer from the outside. When poverty is out of sight, it is easy to ignore it.

Instead of looking at historic and systemic causes of poverty, the poor themselves are blamed. It is almost universal to assume that the poor are lazy, or they just do not try hard enough. Others accuse the poor of being too focused on the moment and failing to make long-term plans. Guilt is easy to excuse when the blame is shifted to the poor.

2

Not All Slums are the Same

Neighborhood design is one of many factors that oppresses the poor and ensures that they remain poor for life. Walking down the street near government housing can be very depressing. The residents have an air of hopelessness about them. The definition of success is to move out. Apathy is the dominant feeling about the neighborhood. Trash is everywhere. Vandalism is a constant problem. These slums hurt the poor and in no way can serve as a model for community design.

Walking down the street of an informal settlement has a completely different feel. The residents are busy trying to earn a living. Home-based stores are everywhere. There is joy, laughter, and most importantly hope.

Why are the residents of one community hopeless and bitter, while those in another are joyful and full of hope? The answer stems from the fact that not all slums are the same. Governmental neglect, ignoring the needs of the poor in community design, oppressive land use laws, violent policing and punishing the poor for takings steps to improve their lives create slums that suck the life out of its residents. Slums that help the poor overcome poverty are created by the freedom of the residents to develop communities that address housing and employment needs along with adequate services.

Types of Slums

The four types of slums are: 1) built for the poor, 2) built for the middle class, 3) built as mixed-income, and 4) built by the poor. The way in which a particular community came into existence largely determines how a slum is categorized. Slum types are important from a design perspective particularly when looking for the features that help the poor overcome poverty.

Built for the Poor Communities

Generally, communities that are built for the poor either warehouse the poor or force them into a middle-class lifestyle. Many of these communities crush the residents by adding to their hardships. These communities reflect the failure of neighborhood design to address the needs of the poor. The residents were not consulted about what neighborhood features meet their needs. A resident in a housing project in East Harlem commented, "Nobody cared what we wanted when they built this place."[10]

Most communities that are built for the poor degrade the residents by making the neighborhood a place to be ashamed of. This leads to a mentality that the residents should make it their goal to move out. Children are taught to study hard so they have a chance to get out. Even state lotteries cash in on convincing the poor to move out. "Ads for the Illinois lottery, posted on billboards in Chicago's poorest neighborhood, read, 'This could be your ticket out.'"[11] No community can help the residents improve their lives when the goal is to move away.

The poor are blamed for not caring about their communities. After all, during times of civil unrest they appear to destroy and burn their own communities. There is no hesitation to loot and burn stores because they are not locally owned so no one knows the owner.[12]

Relocation sites are another form of built for the poor communities. These communities are built for informal settlers whose homes were demolished; hence the name relocation site. The relocation sites around Manila are one-story row houses that look exactly the same. They are built on blocks with roads, not walkways even though none of the residents own cars. Another major flaw of the design is the location. These sites are far from the city so it is literally a drive through farmland and all of a sudden, a huge housing development appears. Families have no choice but to have one member working in the city and coming home every few weeks.

Rita, a resident in an informal settlement in Manila shared about a government project to relocate her community. Many of the residents, including Rita, refused to move. They chose to stay and fight. Rita said, "A friend of mine was relocated but she came back to the city again. The houses there look good, but they are very far from any of the services in the city such as a clinic and even a school. More importantly, there are no jobs. How can we pay our bills if we do not have work? Here in the city we can make money. At least here we live in peace."

With all their flaws, relocation sites have a few positive features. Most importantly, they are built with the idea that the community will improve over time. The residents purchase their home so they are rooted in the neighborhood and have a vested interest in the community. The residents are also allowed to use their homes to run small cottage businesses. While it does take years, some of these neighborhoods are able to become viable communities.

Communities built for the poor, such as public housing are exactly that, housing for the poor. They are not designed to help the poor overcome poverty. The intention is to house people as cheaply as possible so that the upper classes do not have to see poverty.

The issue of slums is much more complex than affordable housing. If that were the only issue, the failed public housing projects that do provide affordable housing for the poor would have been complete successes. Housing vouchers for the poor to live in middle-class neighborhoods would be all that is needed. Urban poverty would no longer be a significant issue. Unfortunately, most built for the poor communities are a huge waste of money and detrimental for the very people they intended to help.

Built for the poor communities contribute to concentrated poverty. The problem with concentrated poverty is not the poor themselves. It is not true that large numbers of poor people in the same area bring each other down in a form of negative synergy. This line of thinking is overstated and victim blaming. The real problem with concentrated poverty is that it exposes the poor to greater levels of oppression. Oppressive community design and policies force the poor to live in specific localities and creates a situation of hopelessness and the related social problems.

One reason why built for the poor communities fail is because people experience the same place differently based on their social class. The same smart growth area that is loved by those who can afford to enjoy the best a city has to offer is at the same time a burden for the poor who are priced out of the area. City planners, architects, and those in political positions to make decisions do not worry about not having enough money to buy groceries for tomorrow's meals. Even if they grew up poor, their current experience is so far removed from the day-to-day realities of poverty that they are not in a position to design a community that meets the needs of the poor.

Built for the Middle Class

Some slums are located in neighborhoods that were originally built as middle-class communities. These neighborhoods are in a season of decline. A community on the decline is often one of hopelessness. Private businesses move out and government services move in. The UN-Habitat offensively refers to this type of community as a slum of despair described as, "'declining' neighborhoods, in which environmental conditions and domestic services are undergoing a process of degeneration."[13] There could be various reasons for this such as the closure of a major employer or political decisions that undercut the community. A community on the decline loses homeowners who fear if they do not get out soon the value of their home will plummet. It creates a "we better take our losses and leave before it gets worse" mentality. Once the cycle of decline gets enough momentum it is very hard to stop a community from continuing the downward spiral of urban decay.

30

Middle-class communities that have transitioned to become slums were designed based on the wants of the middle and upper classes. The amenities meant for the original residents actually cause further hardship for the poor. These neighborhoods were built assuming the occupants would own cars. Now on top of housing expenses the poor also need to own a car to survive.

Built for middle-class slums contribute to the isolation of the poor. Middle and upper class neighborhoods are not designed to enhance relationships. Neighbors do not have many opportunities to naturally meet each other. Relational bonds are very difficult to develop and maintain in these communities.

Another destructive part of built for the middle-class slums are the zoning laws instituted when the community was built as middle-class housing. Forcing the poor to live in residential only neighborhoods greatly hinders their ability to improve their lives. They are stuck in the formal economy, which for the poor means long hours at dead-end minimum wage jobs. It also means that goods and services are not readily accessible. The poor are forced to spend their limited resources to transport groceries and other basic necessities home.

Built as Mixed-Income Communities

The newest trend in policy regarding slums is the push for mixed-income communities. Urban sociologists John Palen writes, "It is assumed that in order to integrate poor inner-city residents into the social and economic fabric of the city, concentrations of the poor either have to be physically dispersed or new mixed-income neighborhoods developed."[14] Mixed-income is an important component for communities that help the poor improve their lives. The major difference between the mixed-income communities currently being built and ones that actually help the poor is how a community becomes mixed-income. A community that helps the poor improve their lives has middle and upper class residents that were formally poor and have chosen to remain in the neighborhood.

Current zoning laws make it impossible to have true mixed-income communities. The only way to have any type of mixed-income is to provide the poor with rent vouchers to be able to live in a middle-class community. This is a cosmetic solution that does not really solve anything.

The HOPE VI program in the US seeks to replace public housing projects with mixed-income communities.

> The HOPE VI Program was developed as a result of recommendations by National Commission on Severely Distressed Public Housing, which was charged with proposing a National Action Plan to eradicate severely distressed public housing. The Commission recommended revitalization in three general areas: physical improvements, management improvements, and social and community services to address resident needs.[15]

The whole purpose of HOPE VI is to eradicate severely distressed public housing. How do you expect to help the poor improve their lives when that is not even the objective? Maybe HOPE VI is not really about helping the poor improve their lives, but an excuse to destroy the homes of the poor and replace them with housing that will earn the government more tax revenues.

One of the major flaws of HOPE VI is that in order to get a wide range of incomes they rely on subsidies and public housing. This is not naturally mixed-income and as the government should have learned from the housing projects that are currently being demolished, it is unsustainable because eventually a future administration will slash the budget.

Mixed-income communities currently being developed lack design features that help the poor improve their lives. They are designed with features that serve the middle class, while the needs of the poor are overlooked.

Built by the Poor

Communities built by the poor are naturally developed. These are mainly informal settlements found in low and middle-income nations. Tent cities in high-income nations are also naturally developed, but because of government persecution, they are rarely able to develop into fully functioning communities.[16] These communities are not places where people fester in their poverty. They are places where residents are struggling their way out of poverty, not out of their communities. Squatter communities, informal settlements, tent cities, or whatever you want to call them are poor people's response to poverty as a way to help them improve their lives.

Tent cities in the US have great potential if they are allowed to develop. The Jungle in San Jose, CA could have been a great place for the poor to overcome poverty had the city not destroyed the community. The residents were well on their way to building a functional community that met their needs.

> The Jungle works for the people who live there, providing a
> sense of community, a support network, even a meager
> livelihood. The Jungle has its own crude system of governance,
> with order often maintained vigilante-style, residents say. 'Any
> time people break the rules, they're asked to leave,' said a
> longtime inhabitant, known as Giggles.[17]

Built by the poor communities can usually trace their history to a few brave people who built a makeshift tent on an unused plot of land. If no one bothers them, a semi-permanent structure will be built using scrap materials. Other families will also move in constructing similar structures. If they are continually left alone, even more improvements will be made. The population will continue to grow as more and more rural poor migrate to the city and move to the community. Eventually enough families will live there that they can petition for government services such as water, electricity, and garbage removal.

When informal settlers are not threatened or hindered by the government they will slowly improve their homes as money becomes available. The exception to this trend is when the residents always have demolition threats hanging over their heads. In this case, their homes will not be improved, and the community will be stuck in one of the early stages of development. Another exception is when building codes forbid the expansion of homes and limit the use of permanent materials. This too causes a community to stagnate.

It is important to note that being left alone does not mean neglected. The gradual transformation of an informal settlement does not rest solely on the residents. Every community needs government services for any hope of improvement. In fact, one form of oppression is withholding services.

The communities of Pook Malinis and Botocan demonstrate how the extent of oppressive policies can impact an informal settlement. These communities are right next to each other in Quezon City. Their immediate proximity makes the case study stronger since the other variables are essentially the same.

Pook Malinis

Pook Malinis is much poorer than its neighboring informal settlements. Although its name means *clean place*, it is anything but clean. This community has a dirt road and a few cemented walkways. The homes are mainly single story wooden structures. Aside from a few small convenient stores in the front window of homes, the only other businesses are shops that purchase recyclables.

The reason why all of the homes are makeshift wooden structures is because the community is under constant intimidation from the landowner who sends armed guards to ensure that the residents do not improve their homes. The residents are told that if they cement their home it will be immediately demolished. They are also forbidden to rent their home. If the

34

landowner finds out that someone is renting they will also be demolished. Thus, the community is stuck in an early stage of development.[18]

Botocan

The bustling community of Botocan was originally a vacant field that was overgrown with grass and weeds. Today the only plants that are left are potted plants on rooftops and a few trees. Most homes are multistory cement buildings, although there are still a few wooden structures.

The residents themselves constructed the houses. Every improvement was a sacrifice. Over time a community was formed. Even to this day, it is common to see home improvement projects going on throughout the community. The people are investing in making their lives more comfortable because they have hope the community will continue to improve.

Even a casual observer can recognize the wide array of businesses within the community. The lines between residential and commercial are blurred into obscurity, as economic activity is practically everywhere. The result is a vibrant community that serves the needs of the residents.

The issues of poverty are the same issues that shaped the design of the community. The residents used the resources they had to build the best they could. The result is a community that addresses the various needs of the residents and helps them overcome poverty.

Politics in Informal Settlements

There are many misconceptions of informal settlements. In informal settlements, the residents do not own the land, but that does not mean they are freeloading off the government. Homes need to be built and maintained. Renters need to keep up on their payments or face eviction.

Informal settlements are not places of anarchy. Behind the seemingly chaotic structure, there is order. If the official government is unable or unwilling to maintain order, the people will organize themselves. This is because society's good and an individual household's good are not always in alignment.

In Botocan there is a fully functioning government with taxes and local elections. Home sales in the community are taxed and businesses have to pay a minimal annual tax. Businesses are also requested to follow citywide business laws such as an ordinance requiring businesses to use paper bags instead of plastic.

Even though the residents do not own the land, they do own their building. Therefore, a home can be sold or rented. As a family becomes more stable, they often build an extra room as a rental unit.

The buildings are not completely unregulated. Houses cannot be expanded into public walkways. However, the second story can extend above the walkway as long as it does not go over a neighbor's house since they may eventually want to build up once they can afford the addition.

One of the striking features of my area in Botocan is how quiet it is at night. I am often disappointed when I travel and stay in hotels because they are usually louder than my home in an informal settlement. This is because the community has a 10 pm noise curfew that neighbors around us follow. I can actually hear insects at night, which is amazing for any urban community, much less a densely crowded slum.

3

New Neighborhood Models are Needed

If a person's home is their castle, then their neighborhood is their kingdom. A kingdom is meant to preserve the life and welfare of the citizens. Likewise, the design of neighborhoods should serve the residents. Ironically, even though every obscure detail is planned, most neighborhoods do not enhance quality of life.

When we look at community design there are several questions we need to ask. Who is being served by the community? Is the community for the maximum profit of the real estate development corporation? What impact does the community have on the surrounding area? What is its ecological footprint? Is it designed to help the residents improve their lives? Does it help neighbors meet each other? Does it take into consideration the needs of children, seniors, and the poor? Is the community walkable, mixed-use, and mixed-income?

Unsustainable Neighborhoods

New neighborhood models are needed because the current ones are unsustainable. A key factor in sustainability is not damaging the environment to the point that it cannot support life. Animal and plant species should not be driven to extinction because of irresponsible growth. Social sustainability is also vital. This recognizes the dangers of marginalizing certain groups within society. Injustice hurts everyone in the end. Oppressed people will eventually fight to challenge the injustice resulting in social unrest.

Environmentally Unsustainable

As the world's population continues to grow, there is an increasing realization that the current situation cannot continue indefinitely. The lifestyle demands of the new middle class across the globe are looking at North Americans and saying, "I want to live like that." Low-density, single-family home communities are popping up around the world as American sprawl serves as the model for neighborhood design.

Given the earth's limited resources we must ask, what is a sustainable neighborhood for everyone on the planet? It is certainly not suburban sprawl. The environmental impact of large single-family homes in residential only communities is much larger than the actual plot of land the house is on. These energy intensive neighborhoods drain resources far and wide.

The environmental consequences of sprawl are well documented. Professors Mark Gottdiener and Leslie Budd write, "Typical suburban sprawl completely destroys water habitats for all species. In many areas of the country, pollution from suburban runoff now exceeds that produced in industry. Floods that were once only decades apart now occur regularly."[19]

The major issue is the need to stop sprawl and push for higher density areas in city centers. Professor Stephen Wheeler writes, "Stabilizing the outward growth of cities and suburbs—and in the process preserving agricultural land, wilderness, important natural habitat, and species—is one of the most pressing challenges for sustainability planning."[20]

Residential only communities, strip malls, and the massive road network needed to connect them consume a staggering amount of land. "The US Department of Agriculture estimates that some two million acres of open space are lost to urbanization annually in the United States."[21] It does not take a rocket scientist to do the math and realize that the current pattern of development is environmentally unsustainable.

Socially Unsustainable

Oppressing, exploiting, and ignoring the poor and marginalized will always come back to haunt a society. History is replete with examples of grass roots uprisings, from ancient civilizations to modern nations. The French Revolution, the anti-apartheid struggle in South Africa, and the civil rights movement in the US are just a few of the better-known examples. Whenever a group of people is marginalized, all of society is at risk.

Richard Wilkinson and Kate Pickett in their book *The Spirit Level: Why Greater Equality Makes Societies Stronger* present research to show that a wide array of social problems are related to social inequality. They write, "Inequality seems to make countries socially dysfunctional across a wide range of outcomes."[22] Neighborhoods that hinder the poor from improving their lives ensure high levels of inequality, and all of the accompanying social problems.

Inequality is compounded by class isolation. Most people do not really know anyone outside of their social class. When people do not actually know someone who is different, they have to look elsewhere to learn about them. This is usually from popular media, which portrays the poor as lazy violent criminals. The middle and upper class assume that the poor do not want to work, have babies to get more welfare, and just do not try hard enough. The poor assume that the rich are snobs who are paid a lot of money to sit at a computer all day. Fear and distrust is the result of class segregation.

Class isolation is not simply a historical phenomenon. It is intentional. The current neighborhood models in the US are based on class segregation that favors the upper classes at the expense of the poor. The poor are priced out of neighborhoods because it is illegal to build a tiny house on a small lot in an area zoned for large luxury homes.

For the most part, zoning laws are legalized class segregation. Zoning laws ensure that the poor are concentrated in certain areas. While zoning laws might be justified for safety, in practice they make sure that the middle and upper classes do not see poor people when they look out their windows. Even though zoning laws are just another name for segregation, and discriminatory, the Supreme Court has yet to find them unconstitutional.

Isolation and separation hurts everyone. It might financially benefit the land owning middle and upper classes, but socially the costs for everyone are high. Racial segregation hurts everyone in society, not just those discriminated against. In the same way, class segregation is also damaging to all of society. We lose part of our own humanity when we are prejudiced against others. The only way to break the vicious cycle of fear and distrust is to develop meaningful relationships with those different from us. The only way to do that is to have open dialogue with one another as human beings. The best way for this to happen is as neighbors, which would mean outlawing class segregation.

Oppression in America's Slums

Most low-income communities in the US are oppressive. They force the poor into dependency and prevent them from improving their lives. Benesh writes, "There are systemic injustices such as corruption, greed, racism, and exclusionary practices that oftentimes become part of the built environment of cities."[23] For the most part, low-income communities in America have failed the residents.

The residents of informal settlements in low and middle-income nations are in some ways better off than those in America's slums. Much of this has to do with the design of informal settlements where residents start their own businesses and are able to survive by their own ingenuity and determination. America's urban poor are punished when they try to start their own business.

Informal settlers have built their own communities that not only meet their housing needs, but also serve as a stepping-stone for getting out of poverty. They occupy land that is not only available, but is also located near places of employment, or at least accessible to public transit. The residents are also not hindered from becoming self-employed. One can enter any decent sized informal settlement and purchase a wide variety of basic goods.

The attitude that if you can't make it in America you can't make it anywhere is deceptive and entirely false. This might be true for those born in a certain income bracket, but for the poor, poverty is often permanent. One of the causes of generational poverty in America is neighborhood design in low-income communities, which is often the result of oppressive zoning policies. These oppressive zoning laws are designed to ensure that the property values of the upper classes are protected without regard to its negative impact on the poor.

Innocent zoning laws that separate residential housing from commercial activity might not appear to be oppressive, but the results are devastating. Single-use zoning is one of the reasons why the American Dream has virtually ended for the poor.

In a low-income neighborhood, a child cannot do her homework because her pencil broke and it would cost her parents at least a dollar in gas just to drive to a giant box store to buy twenty pencils when they only need one. Knowing they do not have enough gas to make a special trip to the store, the parents make the difficult decision of telling their child to do her homework in her head. If their neighbors were allowed to run businesses from their homes, this child would have been able to buy a pencil and completed her homework. In the process she would have contributed to the local economy by helping a neighbor's home-based business.

The United Nations Human Settlements Programme made the following observations regarding oppressive policies related to informal businesses owned by the poor.

In the developed countries, great efforts are made to eliminate the hidden economy since most of the tax base depends upon income tax and value—added tax from formal enterprises, and since many people involved also receive social security. Many developing countries have also regarded the informal sector, just like squatter housing, as something illegal to be exterminated (and something out of which the upper class cannot easily make money and which may even undercut their own legal enterprises). They have therefore harassed the informal sector in a variety of ways.[24]

Low-income communities in the US are not designed to help people get out of poverty. They are designed as if poverty is supposed to be permanent, and function to ensure that it is. Community developer John Perkins writes, "When people have no hope for their community's betterment, or even their personal betterment, it is manifested in many ways. Because there is no vision of ever owning the businesses on their streets or the houses they live in, they see no point in going to school or working."[25] Neighborhoods can and should help families earn livable wages by providing accessibility to employment and the venue to operate small businesses.

Shortcomings in Current Neighborhood Models

Not Child Friendly

Columbia University psychologist Suniya Luthar conducted research among teenagers from upper class suburbs in the US. Her research revealed, "that despite their access to resources, health services, and high-functioning parents, these teens were much more anxious and depressed than teens from inner-city neighborhoods who were faced with all manner of environmental and social ills. The privileged suburban teens smoked more, drank more, and used more hard drugs than inner-city teens."[26] Luthar's findings challenge parents to rethink the type of neighborhood that is really best for children.

A picturesque American Dream neighborhood might not be the best place to raise children. Leigh Gallagher writes, "The wholesale reliance on the car in today's suburbs is especially hard on adolescents, who under this setup need to rely on their parents as chauffeurs until they're sixteen or seventeen. This makes them unnaturally dependent at precisely the moment developmental experts say it's most important for them to become independent."[27]

Most neighborhoods only have a few features for children if any at all. No wonder why some parents have such a hard time getting their children to go outside. There is nothing to do outside and it certainly does not compare with spending all day playing online games. Gottdiener points out the root of the problem when he writes, "Children are actually among the largest consumers of public outdoor environments. Yet, their needs are often ignored by planners and developers."[28]

One of the most important aspects for children is having someone to play with. This is where informal settlements have an advantage. Because of the high-density, there is no shortage of playmates. The parents around me do not have a problem getting their kids to go outside. It is getting them to stop playing and come home that is the problem.

To be sure, some children in informal settlements have a very difficult life. Much of this is directly related to poverty. Hunger, malnutrition, lack of health care, and low quality education are unacceptable injustices against children. Nevertheless these are all symptoms of poverty and not caused by the community.

Some informal settlements can be great places to raise children. Both of my children were born and raised in an informal settlement, and they like it there. The community offers them a seemingly unlimited supply of playmates, safe places to play, stores to walk to, and responsible adults watching them.

When it comes to what is best for children, every neighborhood has room for improvement. It is worth bringing to the design discussion that many upper class communities are not child friendly, while informal settlements offer children places to play and hangout.

Anti-Small Business

Small businesses are extremely beneficial to a community. The owners live locally so they have a vested interest in the welfare of the neighborhood and money spent in their stores stays in the community. In contrast, chain stores could care less about a specific community and money spent there largely leaves the area.

Small locally owned businesses invest in the local community. Political activist David Korten writes, "Local investment provides local employment and produces local goods for local consumption using local resources, the entrepreneur's natural inclination contributes to the vitality of the local economy. And because the owner and the enterprise are both local they are more readily held to local standards."[29]

When the economy is tied to a huge corporation with thousands of employees, one boardroom decision can be devastating to a community. When those jobs are spread out over hundreds of small businesses, there is economic stability. The damage done if a small company decides to move or close is minimal because there are many others in the area.

True market competition is absent in current policy. Even without the tax breaks subsidizing large corporations, low-density residential only neighborhoods favor corporate box stores and online retailers to the detriment of small local businesses. Palen writes, "Population dispersion also puts small, locally owned shops and restaurants out of business and concentrates shopping and dining in national chains."[30] The separation of residential and commercial means that people need to shop online or drive whenever they buy something. In order to accommodate customers who drive, large parking lots are provided. Public roads are built and/or widened so that customers have easy access to do their one-stop shopping.

Single-use neighborhoods discourage small-scale entrepreneurs. Having to rent store space away from one's home in order to start a business significantly increases the costs. The business has to become profitable quickly for a startup to survive. It is impossible to open a business without having a large amount of startup capital or taking on massive debt. The poor are therefore unable to become small business owners. Even if someone is brilliant in terms of business, if they are poor, the odds are stacked against them.

Single-use zoning forces small businesses to operate informally and illegally. While visiting a friend in Lancaster, Pennsylvania I noticed the unusual design of the basement. When I asked about it I learned that the former owners ran a restaurant from the basement. This could have been a great benefit to the neighborhood if they were not forced to keep it a secret. Instead of being thanked for helping the local economy, they risked arrest for illegally selling noodles.

The issue with food is safety. What lawmakers fail to acknowledge is that when you sell to someone that lives near you there is much more pressure to ensure food safety as opposed to a random government inspection. Health inspections are needed for food businesses whose owners are distanced from their business establishment. A small-scale food business run by an owner occupant from their home should be able to operate with less government restrictions and red tape because of the natural social pressure to provide safe food products.

Car Ownership is Needed to Survive

Most communities are designed to sell cars. Roads are the dominant form of public space and parking is plentiful making driving as convenient as possible. Communities designed to sell cars do not help the poor improve their lives. Finding housing options in the US that allow people to entirely give up car ownership are few and far between. Urban planner Jeff Speck writes, "Most American cities have been designed or redesigned principally around the assumption of universal automotive use, resulting in obligatory car ownership, typically one per adult—starting at age sixteen."[31]

The poor are in a Catch-22 in terms of housing options. They need inexpensive housing as well as walkability and access to public transportation. Unfortunately, these are not package deals. More often than not, the poor have to choose one or the other. Inexpensive homes are often located away from urban centers so they lack walkability and public transportation. The inability of the poor to afford homes in walkable neighborhoods forces them to the suburbs where they need to take on the burden of car ownership.

In order to address the poverty caused by requiring car ownership the poor are offered assistance. New moms and their children can qualify for Women, Infants, and Children (WIC) which is basically food vouchers equaling about $100 monthly. It costs several times that much to own and maintain even a clunker of a car. Many families are certainly helped by WIC to meet their nutritional needs, but programs like this would not be as necessary if neighborhood models did not require car ownership for survival. It is interesting how many poor in the US use their car to pick up donated food. This is not a criticism of the poor for buying a car. If they did not own a car, they would not be able to find a job or even get to the store to buy necessities. By making car ownership an essential instead of a luxury, the poor are forced to spend money on car ownership, maintenance, insurance, and gas instead of other more important necessities. Montgomery writes, "The poorest fifth of American families pour more than 40 percent of their income into owning and maintaining cars. When working families move far from their jobs in order to find affordable homes, they can end up blowing their savings just getting there."[32] Car ownership places a huge burden on the poor who are constantly struggling to get a foothold.

The necessity of car ownership did not just happen. The shift from urban to suburban living was not the result of freedom-loving Americans making decisions out of their own free will. The federal government manipulated the population to get them to abandon urban life for low-density, residential only, single-family homes. Gottdiener writes, "Sprawl is planned because it is, in part, the direct result of federal government subsidies that encourage this kind of growth."[33] The two programs responsible for the displacement of the poor and all the tragic consequences of sprawl are the homeowner tax subsidy, and the Federal Aid Highway Act of 1956. These two laws combined gave middle-class families financial incentives to live in the suburbs and the massive road network necessary for sprawl.

President Eisenhower signed the Federal Aid Highway Act of 1956 when Charles Wilson was the Secretary of Defense. Charles Wilson was the CEO of General Motors before becoming Secretary of Defense. After his resignation, he returned to the automobile company to reap the profits from the act.

Federal Aid Highway Act of 1956 provided federal funding for the interstate system in the name of national defense. Linking roads to national defense was a blatant conflict of interest, since the Secretary of Defense had a vested interest in selling cars. The functionality of highways for national defense has yet to be proven. But the highway system does help car sales. Publicly funded highways are billions of dollars in welfare subsidies to the auto industry.

The effects of these government policies on the poor and African-American communities cannot be overstated. Gottdiener writes, "Highway construction has ripped cities apart. More often than not they have destroyed the urban social fabric by cutting neighborhoods into parts that are then isolated from each other."[34]

Building Codes

Building codes have been around for thousands of years. Hammurabi's code, one of the oldest known legal codes, held the builder responsible for the safety and quality of a house.

> If a builder builds a house for a man and does not make its construction sound, and the house which he has built collapses and causes the death of the owner of the house, the builder shall be put to death. If a builder builds a house for a man and does not make its construction sound, and a wall cracks, that builder shall strengthen that wall at his own expense.[35]

Aside from the execution of the builder of a defective house, Hammurabi's code has advantages over modern building codes. Hammurabi's code gave builders the freedom to build houses of any size, shape, color, and material. It just had to be durable and safe.

The law code of the ancient Hebrews listed one regulation related to building new homes. "When you build a new house, you must build a railing around the edge of its flat roof. That way you will not be considered guilty of murder if someone falls from the roof."[36] Ancient Near Eastern rooftops were used as guestrooms and a place to escape the summer heat in the evening. The railing was meant to limit the chances of someone accidently falling off the rooftop.

Ancient building codes were concerned about safety. This should be the concern of modern building codes. Factories need to have multiple fire exits and smoke detectors. Lead-based paint, asbestos, and other toxic materials should not be used. Buildings in earthquake prone areas should be able to withstand an earthquake. Modern fire safety measures that actually prevent fires should be adopted. Common sense safety regulations are important. The problem is that too often building codes have nothing to do with safety.

Cities and counties in the US often require uniform lot and house sizes. Uniform lot sizes do nothing but segregate the population and damage the environment. Many places in the United States even have a minimum house size as part of the building code. Large houses are not simply a fad, but the law. A large house means lots of space that needs to be filled with stuff. It is a way to manipulate Americans to over consume.

Minimum lot and structure requirements hurt the poor. They ensure that there will always be a shortage of affordable housing. If I want to live in a 150 square foot house, I have to find loopholes in the law such as putting it on a trailer and not calling it a permanent residence. An inexpensive, safe, and environmentally friendly home is illegal in many places in the United States.

Building codes cause the poor to suffer because they are prevented from constructing homes that meet their needs. UN Millennium Project Task Force on Improving the Lives of Slum Dwellers came up with similar conclusions when they wrote, "Building bylaws for new settlements prescribe materials and forms of construction that the poor cannot afford."[37]

The safety standards today are based on the concept of making a structure with maximum safety and minimum materials. For a home developer this is ideal because it allows homes to be built as cheaply as possible. There are however, other measurements to use as the basis of safety codes. Instead of minimum materials, safety ordinances can be designed for maximum safety with 100% recycled material, or only using local materials. There are many ways to achieve the objective of a structurally safe home. Building codes oppress the poor when they legalize only one way and discredit all the other ways to make a building safe.

Zoning Laws

Freedom loving Americans live under massive government control and regulations. The lack of freedom is seen in the way cities are developed. Montgomery writes, "The vast majority of cities in the developed world have been shaped by rules that might already be considered totalitarian for the level of control they exert."[38] Zoning laws specify how a certain area of land is to be used, the specifics regarding any buildings on the land, and the absolute separation of housing, employment, and stores. Zoning laws and building codes determine housing choices in America.

One form of oppression is thwarting the efforts of the poor to improve their lives. Zoning laws that criminalize the efforts of the poor to improve their lives by banning home-based businesses are oppressive.

Zoning laws originally came as a response to the health crisis caused by the Industrial Revolution. The desire was to move residential housing away from factories that pumped toxic fumes into the air. In many ways, they are a carryover from a past era. Montgomery writes, "These days such geometrically pure separatist schemes have lost much of their health-related raison d'être. With the help of emission controls and sewage systems, city centers in most advanced economies are no longer toxic, at least in the physical sense. But the ideology of separation has lived on."[39] Naturally, no one wants to live next to a smoke filled factory, but that is no longer the issue.

Some zoning laws are for health and safety. I have lived next to a gas station, nightclub, and restaurant so I know what it is like to live with noise and light pollution as well as unpleasant smells. Noise and odor concerns are legitimate, but they cannot be so rigid that all businesses are banned from operating next to where people live. Noise and smells are also in purely residential neighborhoods. Even the residents in elite gated subdivisions are disturbed by the noise from lawnmowers. Homes located in the country far away from neighbors have the noise of nature, which can also be loud. Smells are the same way. Anyone who has lived on a farm knows that fresh country air is really the smell of manure.

Zoning laws need to distinguish between unpleasant odors and toxins. Factories that pump toxins into the air must be regulated. Factories that would be health hazards for a community should be required to limit the amount of toxins released, and to clean up their mess. When the public is at risk of being poisoned because of someone's greed, the government has the responsibility to have safety legislation in place. Isolating factories from residential areas is not the solution because it just allows destructive businesses to continually destroy the environment unchecked.

Toxins are not an issue of home-based businesses because the owner/occupant will be the first to suffer. Most home-based businesses are entirely odor free. Since the building also serves as the owner's home they are not going to stink up the place. Even those with slight odors, the smells are entirely harmless, and in many cases appealing as in the pleasant smell of baking bread.

The argument of safety is lost when the rules become so nitpicky that one has to wonder what exactly is the health hazard that the law is intended to address. Urban planner Jeff Speck writes, "Cities are organized not according to 'planning regulations' but by 'zoning codes,' and different land uses still tend to be kept apart much more than health, safety, or common sense would dictate."[40] As an example the stated purpose of the city of Rockwood's zoning laws is to regulate "the use of land, buildings and structures to promote the public health, safety and general welfare."[41] Among the ways that Rockwood intends to promote the health, safety, and welfare of its citizens is through single-use zoning explained as, "dwellings are not permitted in office, commercial or industrial districts."[42] The citizens of Rockwood are not allowed to live next to their office building or stores, because that is somehow detrimental to their health, safety, and general welfare. Instead of being able to walk to work or shop they face the financial burden of car ownership, contribute to environmental degradation, and risk death and injury by driving everywhere.

Rockwood is not unique in its approach to zoning. It is really anywhere that uses generic single-use zoning in the name of public safety. It is actually quite sad that the health, safety, and general welfare of the public are used to justify laws that favor the property values of middle and upper class homeowners at the expense of the poor.

Americans are not the only ones who suffer because of our zoning laws. UN Millennium Project Task Force on Improving the Lives of Slum Dwellers determined that, "City planning bylaws and zoning regulations in low-income countries are derived mainly from experience in developed countries. As such, they are anti-pedestrian, anti-street, and anti-mixed land use—in short, against all the things that are compatible with the priorities and realities of low-income groups."[43] Instead of other countries copying American sprawl, America needs to study how the world's poor build communities to meet their needs. America's poor would be greatly served if city planners and local politicians took lessons from the wisdom of informal settlers in low-income countries.

Where zoning laws need to be reconsidered is the extent to which they hinder the poor from homeownership, prevent all commercial activity next to housing, and are detrimental to quality of life. All these situations are damaging. Neighborhood models must address the need for the poor to be able to afford homeownership and engage in business.

Property Value Trumps All

It is easy to understand why homeowners want some assurance that their home will not lose value. Houses are the largest investment for the middle class. The investment is so large that home mortgages are usually 30 years. This means that the majority of someone's working life is spent paying off their home mortgage.

One risk of homeownership is that the value of a home is influenced by what goes on in the area around the property. A major employer deciding to leave, declining public schools, or a recession can all lower property values. Homebuyers' risk having to pay off a mortgage that is more than the house is worth.

The real purpose of zoning laws is to help assure homeowners that neighbors will not jeopardize property values. Montgomery writes, "Zoning was intended to reduce congestion, improve health, and make business more efficient. But most of all, it protected property values. Perhaps this is why we so enthusiastically embraced it."[44] By giving homeowners control over what neighboring property can be used for, they have some security that their home will maintain its value. The system is not foolproof as was demonstrated by the 2008 housing market crash.

Property value has become so important that it trumps everything else. It is even more important than diversity and free market. Segregation and diversity cannot coexist. The high value for diversity found in many areas of the US ignores class diversity. A bunch of wealthy people hanging out together is not true diversity regardless of how colorful the group might look. Anyone claiming to value diversity should put their money where their mouth is and help work to outlaw class segregation.

Zoning laws are so socialist that Karl Marx might not even approve. The issue with many zoning laws and building codes is that they go way beyond the bounds of acceptable governmental oversight. The government should not have the right to dictate exactly how someone should use his or her land. Yes, there should be some government oversight, but forbidding someone to sell shoes or tee shirts from their home is an affront to free market. The fear of the loss of property values because of mixed-use is so ingrained in our minds that it is hard to imagine how good life can be in a mixed-use community.

It is true that the free market gives unrestrained opportunities to exploit the poor. However, regulations in general are not guarantees that the poor will be protected. Government should be about protecting the most vulnerable citizens from oppression, not making oppressive laws. The sad case of history shows that most laws favor the wealthy and those with power at the expense of the poor and powerless.

New Urbanism

New Urbanism is gaining popularity as a response to the current failed neighborhood models. New Urbanism seeks to go back to the way that cities used to be built and design neighborhoods based on that model. Therefore, walkability and mixed-use are important components in New Urbanism neighborhoods. New Urbanism is doing great work in changing zoning laws to allow mixed-use neighborhoods. Of all the neighborhood models used today, New Urbanism is certainly one of the best.

New Urbanism varies depending on how much of the concept a city or county adopts. Sometimes New Urbanism neighborhoods do a great job at creating a sustainable and livable community. Other neighborhoods that claim to be designed based on New Urbanism ideas are nothing more than a typical sprawl community with a bike path so that it is claimed to be walkable, or it is located behind a strip mall so it is promoted as mixed-use.

Another shortcoming of some New Urbanism developments is that it is still based on control. Entire neighborhoods and in some cases, mini cities are planned and built by a single developer. The community is claimed to be mixed-use, but the developer simply preplans the type and location of businesses. The residents who will live in the neighborhood are not participants in the design of their community, nor can they open a business from their home.

The major flaw of New Urbanism is that, so far, these communities are only for the rich. The price range to live in a New Urbanism neighborhood is barely affordable for the middle class. The poor are left to continue to suffer under the current failed neighborhood model.

Part II

Positive Design Features of Informal Settlements

Informal settlements, while far from perfect, contribute to the welfare of the residents. The residents used what they had and built a community directly around their needs. Over time the neighborhood begins to grow into something beautiful. These neighborhoods are walkable, mixed-use, and mixed-income. They provide housing, employment, and companionship in what would otherwise be unbearable circumstances.

Informal settlements are not some fantasy utopia where the poor all live in harmony. The pain of poverty, oppression, and injustice are real. Whole books can be written describing some of the horrors of poverty. However, there is another story. In order to see the positive features of informal settlements it is necessary to separate poverty from the community itself. When we do this, a new picture emerges of beauty and hope as the poor improve their lives.

The beauty and hope within informal settlements is there, we just need to take off the blinders that have conditioned us to see informal settlements as problems. Even some low-income communities in the US have aspects that we can learn from. After visiting a slum in Boston, Jane Jacobs commented, "You should have more slums like this . . . You ought to be down here learning as much as you can from it."[45] It is time that slums are studied not for their problems, but for what we can learn from them. Can some slums really serve as a model for neighborhood design? Absolutely! Jane Jacobs believed they could, and she is far from alone.

In many respects, informal settlements are better than most planned neighborhoods because the needs of the residents themselves are the basis for how they are developed. Botocan has what many other well-planned neighborhoods either totally lack or attempt to have but can never quite figure out. Botocan is walkable and has easy access to public transportation. The community is an authentic mixed-use and mixed-income neighborhood as residential and commercial flourish right next to each other. The result is a vibrant community that addresses the needs of the poor and helps them overcome poverty. These concepts will be examined in detail in part two of this book.

4

Land Use Freedom

Informal settlements are developed from the ground up based on the needs of the residents. Land is utilized in ways that are most useful for residents at the time. Private buildings can be used for housing, a business, or both and can change with the changing needs of households. Public space can also change its main function, or be converted into private lots.

Compared to residential only housing projects, Botocan is significantly more sustainable and livable. Residential only slums lack private businesses and are full of government services providing enough assistance to survive but not enough to help the residents overcome poverty. The residents are caught up in a system that places a social worker in power over them. Poverty is disempowering and dehumanizing.

Botocan on the other hand is a place of opportunity and hope. The formal sector does not provide enough jobs for the residents, but instead of being forced to rely on government handouts, the people are free to create their own employment. The community design gives the residents the freedom to find creative ways to improve their lives. They can maintain their dignity as they provide for their families through home-based businesses.

Mixed-Income

Informal settlements are first and foremost people's homes and businesses. On the outside, they might not look nice, but that does not mean they are bad places to live. The false assumption is that "everywhere their function is the same: to house those who have the least resources and nowhere else to go."[46] It is true that many people who live in informal settlements do not have many resources, but certainly not everyone. Another misunderstanding in this statement is that informal settlements only serve the housing needs of the poor. Informal settlements meet a variety of needs, which is why they help the poor improve their lives and overcome poverty.

There are a number of residents in Botocan that do have a choice regarding housing, and they choose to stay. Botocan has a relatively large income differentiation among the residents. The highest monthly income per household is P68,000 ($1,360 US)[47] and the lowest is 3,000 ($60 US).[48] The monthly income of the highest earner is 22 times that of the lowest. There are families that are very poor. On the other hand earning $1,360 monthly in the Philippines is deep into middle-class income levels.

The highest income earner has an office job. The family chooses to stay in Botocan because the neighborhood is their home. Their friends and family live in Botocan, and they own their home. There is no logical reason for them to move to a neighborhood where they do not know anyone and have to pay expensive rental rates, which would eat up much of their monthly earnings.

Directly related to the income variation is the broad range of employment. It seems as if people from Botocan work everywhere. I have ridden in taxis only to discover that the driver is from Botocan. Sales clerks in stores, the cashier in the grocery store, our oldest son's second grade teacher, and the nurse who attended the birth of our youngest child all live in Botocan.

The residents in Botocan work at a variety of jobs because the community has a broad range of educational levels. The far extremes are those who have never even been to school and others with master's degrees. A small handful of people are illiterate, while others are avid readers.

The housing stock is what allows Botocan to be mixed-income. There are single-story unfinished houses with scrap wood for walls. The other extreme are three-story homes with rooftop decks and beautiful interiors. Some are so spacious and well maintained that it is easy to forget that you are actually in an informal settlement.

Jane Jacobs argues that, "Cities need old buildings so badly it is probably impossible for vigorous streets and districts to grow without them."[49] The importance of old buildings is that they provide cheaper rents than new ones. In other words, communities need diversified rental options.

The rental units available in Botocan are another indication that the community is truly mixed-income. The rental rates start at P1,000 ($20 US) per month. This will provide a family with a small room and a shared bathroom. The most expensive rental that I have seen is a house for P7,500 ($150 US) per month. This is a three-room home complete with a kitchen, bathroom, and a small deck. The home is quite impressive considering it is in an informal settlement. The most expensive rental unit is 7.5 times more than the cheapest. The equivalent of this rental range in the US would be $200 to $1,500. If American neighborhoods could match this rental range, they too would truly have mixed-income communities.

Mixed-income neighborhoods provide social diversity that is beneficial for both the low and high-income earners in the neighborhood. On the practical level, those residents with social connections can help others find employment and provide a voice that government officials will listen to. Mixed-income allows a community to have a wide variety of job skills. When our water pipe broke and was literally spraying water everywhere it was just a matter of minutes before we were able to find a skilled plumber who was able to fix the problem immediately.

Social class diversity provides the opportunity for beautiful relationships. My family and I often have neighbors over for meals. Some of them would not eat otherwise. Sometimes they will do the dishes and help in other ways around the house. This is not a business transaction since we never verbally agree on an exchange. We simply offer what we have in the form of an invitation to share a meal together and in return, they often do the dishes without even asking. This is an example of friends sharing life together across social class.

Mixed-Use

Max Weber in his classic *The City* views a city as a place, "where the local inhabitants satisfy an economically substantial part of their daily wants in the local market, and to an essential extent by (sic) products which the local population and that of the immediate hinterland produced for sale in the market or acquired in other ways. In the meaning employed here the 'city' is a market place."[50] The idea of a city as a local market is an image of mixed-use. In informal settlements the poor are able to have much of their daily wants satisfied in the local "market." The local market of course is the entire mixed-use community.

Slums by their very nature are mainly residential. The area would not be a slum if it were mainly businesses. Yet one of the dominant features of many informal settlements is their strong business sector. Gottdiener writes, "Many shanty towns support robust economies in themselves including areas of real estate investment. They often are the location for small-business enterprises started by urban migrants. Shanty towns may also be the sites for small and medium-sized factories."[51]

The majority of those living in informal settlements do not necessarily want to engage in business. However, all of the residents benefit from the goods and services made available from home-based businesses. Simply having the option to start a business gives residents more control over their lives. It provides the option to have some income while looking for other employment.

Self-employment is a way for the poor to take concrete steps to improve their lives. Social researcher Elisea Adem writes, "These 'do-it-yourself' activities cushion them against joblessness, underemployment, and inflationary cost of living."[52] The ability to operate a business from their home is vital for poor entrepreneurs. The United Nations Human Settlements Programme determined that, "Without the ability to make a living that working in the home or street provides, many households would be in dire straits. Indeed, without the ability to run a business without paying for a specific building, much larger profits would be required for liquidity, let alone profit."[53] Informal settlements are true mixed-use communities, meaning the building occupants are free to engage in business from their homes.

Director of African Centre for Cities Edgar Pieterse writes of the need for mixed-use freedom in South Africa.

> The government is confronted by the dilemma that people who have been awarded a 'free' house with basic services by the government sell it way below the value at the moment of transfer, only to return to an informal settlement, because they need some financial liquidity to carry out trading that can only be done in an informal setting as the land-use and property regulations are too restrictive in formal townships.[54]

The poor need the freedom to engage in self-employment activities for their very survival. The South African government's dilemma is easily solved if the homes they build for the poor are designed to be mixed-use so the residents can engage in home-based businesses.

There are about 1,300 structures in Botocan and the vast majority of them are residential. Only a small handful of buildings are purely commercial. Most of the businesses operate directly from the home. Stay-at-home parents can tend to their store while they are watching their children and doing household chores.

There is no major employer inside the community. Botocan is full of small locally owned shops and businesses. Walking through Botocan and literally counting the number of businesses, I found that there are at least 300 small businesses. The exact number of businesses is impossible to determine because they are constantly opening and closing. Many businesses are permanent, while some are seasonal. In the summer, households with refrigerators will sell ice and frozen snacks from their home. Others will sell popular fruit shakes from their front door. During Christmas time, everyone seems to be open for business. Families will set up a table in front of their home and sell toys, clothing, and food.

Most are general stores selling snacks and everyday food items, but some are specialized outlets such as hardware, school supplies, or clothing. There are also two small open-air markets selling fresh produce, meat, and fish. Other shops sell prepared food including several bakeries that serve fresh bread daily. There are service related businesses including a small engine repair shop, water purification, appliance repair, barbershops, Internet cafés, clothing alterations, and cobblers who can fix any kind of footwear.

There are also small-scale manufacturing businesses. This is mostly the tedious work of cutting labels or sewing decorations on clothing. Others manufacture soap or print tee shirts. All of these operate on an as needed basis and serve to supplement the families' income.

The poor are very creative in their businesses. Almost every skill is turned into a way to earn money. There are beauticians and masseuses that are on call and do home service. A sewing machine and years of self-training has enabled one senior to run a sewing and alteration business from his home.

Business investment and personal use are very blurred. A bicycle is used by the family, but also rented to children. In the summer, many families set up inflatable swimming pools and charge a small entrance fee. At least two homemade pool tables are available for rent in Botocan. A home computer and a printer are all a household needs to open a computer shop for students to type and print their homework. A digital camera and a printer allows one family to offer id and passport photos.

Families can easily open and close their stores when their situation changes. One family opened their store because their oldest child started college and they needed the extra income. A different family closed their store when they had another child because they needed the extra space.

The business model at work in Botocan is a form of capitalism that views others as neighbors not competitors. The owners know each other so no one is trying to put others out of business. The stores develop customer loyalty based on relationships and are not seeking to take customers from other businesses. Because of this mindset, a large number of small businesses are able to be a vital source of income for families.

A distinct and very important feature of most businesses in Botocan is that they are not intended to be the family's only source of income. While there are a few businesses that do fully support entire households and even hire employees, most simply supplement the salaries of family members who have other employment. This feature allows businesses to stay open even with relatively low profits. The whole point is to give those who remain at home the chance to earn a little extra. Even if a store only earns enough to cover one of the family's meals each day, that in itself makes a huge difference for the poor. Businesses with relatively small profits can bring stability to an impoverished family.

How a specific building is used is mainly up to the owner, but there are some regulations. The major constraint is the degree to which the use disturbs neighbors. Most are willing to be inconvenienced since the business is used for the livelihood of the household. This situation is vastly different from a large business whose multi-millionaire owner does not live anywhere near their noisy and smelly factory.

Businesses that are illegal everywhere else in the city or harmful to the community are not allowed. Someone cannot open a nightclub, brothel, or a factory that continually pumps out toxic smoke day and night. The oil wells in Los Angeles are a good example of what would not be allowed in Botocan.

Not every business is beneficial to the community. There are three government sponsored lottery stalls sucking money out of the neighborhood. Outsiders making money off the poor own a few businesses inside the community. These are better than chain stores, but only in the sense that they provide a service and save the residents from having to spend money to commute to a store. A lot of junk food is sold to kids and the main way that many stores make their money is by selling alcohol and cigarettes. The easy access to unhealthy products contributes to some of the social and health problems of the residents. Flaws and all, overall the community is better off because there are local businesses.

The huge number of local businesses in Botocan stands in striking contrast to communities that ban business activity in residential neighborhoods. In the United States one of the dominant features of public housing and so-called mixed-income communities is the absence of legal businesses. It is wrong to assume that the poor in America are just not business minded. Low-income neighborhoods would see a vast increase in small business enterprises if land use zoning did not discourage the entrepreneurial-minded poor. The poor would work their way into a more secure and stable life.

Benefits of Residential with Business Opportunities

Mixed-use communities provide many benefits for the residents. The natural human existence is to live in the same proximity as commercial activities. This makes jobs, goods, and services readily available. Wheeler writes, "Adding residents, jobs, and businesses to a neighborhood provides many advantages, including improving safety; increasing the viability of local businesses, cafés, and restaurants; providing sufficient ridership for transit; enhancing community interaction; and saving open space."[55]

In low-income communities, the presence or absence of locally owned businesses is the key distinction between a slum where residents are overcoming poverty and one where they are trapped under oppressive structures. Locally owned businesses are vital for the poor. Adem writes, "Petty as they are, these small activities are ingenious ways of surviving; and at the same time they are a noble service to the community members in need of the service."[56]

Mixed-use neighborhoods keep money in the community. When I buy freshly baked bread each morning, the money goes to the owner-operator who lives in Botocan. They use some of that money to pay their four employees who also live in the neighborhood. Since everyone associated with the bakery is local, they also shop locally. While money does leave the community for business supplies and people do shop outside, enough money stays locally to create a strong internal economy.

Mixed-use communities can help the small businesses of the poor become profitable quickly. If the poor can operate a business from their home, they can be freed from the major expense of renting commercial space. These communities also provide a strong base of potential customers within walking distance.

Globally engaging in business is one way that the poor overcome poverty. The self-employment model of poverty reduction is where informal settlers excel. They use their skills and creativity to supplement their family's income through home-based businesses.

The business capacity of the poor depends on the ease of a startup. Economist Hernando de Soto comments, "In Peru, informality has turned a large number of people into entrepreneurs, into people who know how to seize opportunities by managing available resources, including their own labor, relatively effectively."[57] The poor in informal settlements must rely on their own ingenuity to survive. When businesses are legalized and the poor are able to earn from their homes the opportunities are almost endless.

Public Space

Communities that enhance quality of life need more than housing and businesses. Public space is a vital component of neighborhoods. Benesh writes, "The power of spaces, whether for good or for bad, directly impacts how people live and function in the city, how people engage with one another (if they do), and even how happy people are in the city."[58]

At its best, public space brings people together and provides a place for residents to build relationships with one another. Public space provides a venue for athletic events and other recreational activities. These can be organized sports leagues, or simply pick-up games. Public space can also be used for expressions of culture and building public awareness through the hosting of a variety of events.

Public space does not automatically improve a community. In fact, in some neighborhoods the local park is the most dangerous place to go. Dead neighborhoods have dead parks, while vibrant neighborhoods have vibrant parks. Jane Jacobs observed, "Too much is expected of city parks. Far from transforming any essential quality in their surroundings, far from automatically uplifting their neighbourhoods, neighbourhood parks themselves are directly and drastically affected by the way the neighbourhood acts upon them."[59] A vibrant public space that is heavily used is dependent on a community that is also full of life.

Botocan has an amazing use of public space. There are two full basketball courts and two smaller half courts. Rain or shine, basketball games are played throughout the day. The backboards and rims are well worn from all the use. The basketball courts serve the community by providing much more than a basketball court. The main court also has a stage, a chapel, and security offices. The only road into the community passes right through the court so all of the pedestrians, bikes, scooters, and tricycles[60] going through Botocan share the public space with everyone else using the court. On Sunday morning, the court is turned into a temporary chapel. Government sponsored programs and meetings are held there. The court is regularly turned into a makeshift clinic for medical check-ups. Celebrations such as birthdays and wedding receptions are also held at the court. The basketball court also serves as the community's garbage collection site. The same public space is sometimes simultaneously used for various distinct purposes. I have seen birthday parties and funerals held next to each other while children are shooting baskets and playing tag. People are buying hamburgers and drinks from courtside shops while chatting with friends.

The main basketball court is where many people congregate, making it a prime business location. There are currently two hamburger stalls, a bakery, a school supply shop, several variety shops, and an Internet café surrounding the court. There are also makeshift shops including an elderly woman who sets up her fruit and peanut table every afternoon. Storeowners' risk having a basketball hit their business in exchange for a prime location for sales.

The basketball court is used almost all the time. Even in the middle of the night there are still a few people outside. The major use starts before 6 am on weekdays with the morning rush of people going to work or school while local shop owners begin setting up for the day. The most use is in the evening until about 9 pm when things start to wind down.

The mixed usage of public space as seen in Botocan and many other informal settlements is exemplary. The space is heavily used by a wide variety of the residents. There are events for everyone throughout the week.

Public space and small businesses thrive with diversity. The greater variety of people in a neighborhood the more public space will be used throughout the day and for different reasons. Small businesses are able to take advantage of the various tastes of the residents adding to the vibrancy of the community.

The basketball court is maintained and operated by the local government. Homeowners directly on the court will also clean parts of the area as needed.

Official reservations to use the court or the stage for special events must be made through the local government for a small fee.

Features that Enable Mixed-Use

Mixed-use is vital for a community to help the poor overcome poverty. In order for a community to be mixed-use, it must have the legal structure to allow for flexible land use, a healthy population density, and be mixed-income.

Flexible Land Use

One of the key features of land use in Botocan is that a specific structure is not locked into its use. The bedroom of a neighbor has a menu painted on the wall. When I asked about it I discovered that the room was once a small restaurant. When the mother was able to find permanent employment, they decided to close the restaurant so that the children could use the space as their bedroom.

Throughout its history, the land use in Botocan has changed and will continue to change in the future. The original residents had small gardens. Coming from the countryside it was only natural to grow vegetables and remain connected to their agricultural roots. As the population grew and space became more of a concern, households started converting their gardens into extra rooms for their growing families. Culturally they were also becoming more urbanized with a new generation born in the city that does not know rural life. The gardens phased out when the residents began to look for other land uses that would address their current needs.

Years ago there was a fishpond in Botocan. This was eventually filled in and converted to a basketball court. That area is still referred to as "fishpond." The need for housing and a basketball court outweighed the need for the fishpond. By that time, it was too polluted and overfished to serve the community. Standing water also creates a breeding ground for mosquitoes. The basketball court that replaced the fishpond remained dirt and gravel for years. Eventually a politician seeking votes had the court paved and another politician installed a roof.

The fluid nature of land use in Botocan is one of the keys to how the community helps its residents improve their lives. As soon as a business opportunity presents itself, someone jumps on the chance. Businesses are able to adjust quickly to the changing needs and tastes of customers.

Healthy Population Density

Healthy population density is vital for communities. A community needs enough people for there to be a solid tax base to fund government programs and for businesses to have enough of a customer base to be profitable.

A healthy population density often means high-density. This should not to be confused with overcrowding. Slums are often associated with overcrowding and the related health and social problems. Overcrowding is an issue for specific households but not entire communities. Overcrowding and depopulation can happen simultaneously. Families can be evicted and the house remain vacant since the owner thinks they can eventually earn more by simply sitting on the property as opposed to renting it at a lower rate. When this happens some people will move away reducing the total population of the area. However, others will move in with relatives on the same block causing that home to be overcrowded. Jane Jacobs observed, "The overcrowded slums of American real life are, more and more typically, dull areas with a low density of dwellings."[61]

Botocan has just over 8,000 people and 1,300 buildings on about 20 acres of land. This is approximately 400 people and 65 buildings per acre. Botocan's buildings are between one to three stories high. The upper stories are often separate units, so the owner can occupy one of the floors and rent out the others.

Botocan's high population density does cause some problems that need to be addressed to better help the poor overcome poverty. The extremely close living conditions allow diseases to easily spread. Privacy is also limited as neighbors hear each other's conversations and family arguments.

Fire is another concern. In March 2018, a fire swept through a section of Botocan and destroyed about 150 homes but did not cause any serious injury or death. Since that time, Botocan has been in a season of rapid rebuilding. Most of the families have rebuilt using concrete blocks and other nonflammable materials in an effort to make the community safer.

There is a positive side to close living conditions. If someone is in trouble, neighbors can easily hear and come to help. A wealthy woman whose husband died of a heart attack told me that if they lived in an informal settlement instead of a gated subdivision her husband would still be alive. In a densely crowded informal settlement, neighbors would have heard him fall and came to his aid. As it turned out, he died because neighbors were too far away to know that he needed help.

High-density is often a positive aspect in an urban setting. Community Resources and Development director Mark Roseland writes, "Denser land use could help solve many of the environmental, social, and aesthetic problems of sprawl."[62] High-density areas are very efficient in terms of services. The fact that there is less space between houses also means that there are less roads, electrical wires, and water pipes. Having fewer roads has a multiplying effect because not only is it cheaper to pave and maintain a shorter distance, it also frees up land that can be used in other ways.

Communities with high-density reduce the number of vacant lots and abandoned buildings being used for drugs and prostitution. Within Botocan, there are no vacant lots. Every square foot of land has some purpose. This contributes to the overall safety of the community.

Another important feature of Botocan's high-density is that it does not feel overly crowded. I rode a train with a young man who spent a month with us in Botocan. During the train ride, he started to get nervous and said that he was claustrophobic because the train was too crowded. Interestingly, in

Botocan he never complained about feeling like there were too many people around.

A Healthy Mix

Neighborhoods should offer residents everything they need in their day-to-day lives. This feature serves all of the city's residents, but is particularly needed by the poor. This is because the poor need employment options near their homes. "Livelihood means jobs close enough to decent housing with wages commensurate with rents and access to the services that make for a healthful habitat. Livelihoods must also be (environmentally) sustainable."[63] The healthy mix of uses, incomes, and walkability naturally within informal settlements meets all of these needs.

The ability to purchase basic goods and attend social activities without transportation costs can greatly increase the disposable income of the poor. There needs to be housing, but also shops to pick up groceries to cook dinner. Not everyone likes to cook so restaurants serving a variety of prepared food are also needed. Children need school supplies and light bulbs burn out so variety stores are needed to provide these essentials. People get headaches and their hair gets too long so they need drug stores, barbershops and beauty parlors. People want to practice their faith so they need places to gather to worship. All of these activities and more are possible in Botocan.

Botocan has a healthy mix of business activity within a mainly residential community that mixed-use advocates in the US can only dream about. This is made possible by being a true mixed-use mixed-income community. Oppressive zoning laws that limits land use do not burden the neighborhood. The residents are free to use their homes in ways that best meet their needs, including commercial activity. This provides a platform for the poor to overcome poverty and improve their quality of life.

5

Public, Private, and Non-Profit Involvement

The type and amount of public, private, and non-profit involvement plays a huge factor in the development of a community and whether or not it will oppress or serve the residents. At minimum, residents need services that are already provided in wealthy communities such as sewage, water, and electricity. The government also needs to provide infrastructure, public education, as well as police and fire departments. When public, private, and non-profits work in alignment with the local residents, communities can be developed in ways that help the residents out of poverty.

Private, Public, and Non-Profit Involvement in Informal Settlements

Private

The private sector plays the main role in the development of informal settlements. The residents build their own houses and contribute to the development of public space and walkways. They also organize a governing body to set rules as needed and to work with the official government to get basic services.

Botocan was built by literally hundreds of private households, not a development corporation. It was the money, sweat, blood, and ingenuity of the residents that built the neighborhood. The original residents suffered through fears of demolition and not having basic sanitation. As the demand for land increased, the right to use the land was a first come first serve basis.

Families built as quickly as possible, and if they did not have the money to build, they put a bench and a rope to stake a claim on the land.

The homes are constantly improving. Permanent structures replaced makeshift tents. For years, wood was the building material of choice. In the event of demolition, wood and nails can be salvaged. The combination of confidence that the government will not evict the residents and the fear of fire has led many homeowners to replace wooden homes with cement. These homes are sturdy and fireproof, but the materials cannot be salvaged if the community is demolished.

The private sector beyond the local residents has both helped and exploited the people. The private sector consists of for-profit businesses. They willingly provide a service as long as it is profitable for their business.

The private sector also provides many employment opportunities. There are private businesses inside and all around the community. Each of these is an opportunity for employment. Some people are forced to work for very low wages at exploitative companies. Other residents are able to secure stable employment at fair wages.

Public

The public sector responds to informal settlements in three different ways. One is to fight the residents and destroy their homes. This response views informal settlements as problems that need to be eliminated. Instead of eliminating poverty, it forces the poor to move and makes their lives worse. The goal is to get rid of the poor so they become someone else's problem.

Another response is to do nothing. The government knows the poor are there but they neither hinder nor help the residents. This is a pure laissez-faire approach and constitutes neglect on the part of politicians. Yes, they are not directly hindering the efforts of the poor to make their neighborhood better, but by not providing basic services the government is in effect slowly but surely destroying the community. Professor of Community

Transformation Randy White writes, "Many studies have examined how neglect has been a strategy of the powerful for economic gain in cities."[64] Neglect is a form of oppression that ensures low-income communities do not improve.

The last way that governments can respond to the efforts of the poor to make their own community is to walk alongside them and assist them by providing services that are the right of every citizen. This helps the poor and serves the greater good of society.

The development of Botocan has been a mix of hindering, helping, and neglect. Even though there are oppressive policies and withholding of services, there have also been some examples of involvement that has truly helped the residents improve their lives.

Botocan is recognized by the government and receives funding from the city. The boundaries include the entire informal settlement, several blocks of an elite gated subdivision, and a large police station. The city government allocates money to each neighborhood based on their property taxes. This means that wealthy communities receive significantly more funds than low-income communities do. When a community's boundaries only include a specific informal settlement, they receive very little government funding. In areas where the informal settlement is only a small part of the community and therefore not significantly represented in the local government, the poor are ignored. In Botocan's case, the local government officials are entirely from the informal settlement. The community also receives a significant budget from the city government thanks to the wealthy residents in the neighboring subdivision.

Currently, 48 government employees work directly in Botocan. This includes elected officials, security guards, street sweepers, and office staff. These government employees serve in a variety of capacities focusing on areas such as education, health, and youth.

Years ago, Botocan had the reputation of being a violent community. Several killings took place in broad daylight. The local government hired local residents to serve as security guards. They carry handcuffs, a nightstick, and a flashlight. The security guards patrol the community all the time and help make Botocan a safe place to live.

The security guards do not have the authority of the police, but they can make arrests and turn someone over to the police. Whenever there is a fight and someone calls the security, they will come and defuse the situation. Abused women have been able to get protection, and drunken neighbors yelling at night are asked to quiet down or risk having to spend the night in a holding cell.

The local government is involved in other areas as well. They provide a trash truck three times a week to collect garbage free of charge. They also hire residents to sweep the walkways every morning. Botocan is amazingly clean considering its population density. There are cities in the United States that have significantly more trash on the streets than in Botocan.

The government also provides a variety of technical skills training seminars free of charge. Some of the recent ones have been classes on how to give massages and cell phone repair. The government also sponsors the high school equivalency exam preparation course.

The government provides a variety of medical services throughout the year such as eye exams, dental check-ups, wellness check-ups for children, and occasionally specialized services. The local government has a vehicle that can be used for emergencies such as taking a pregnant woman to the delivery room. The local government also helps with the medical expenses of the poorer residents by connecting the residents to funders, or by requesting a discount from the hospital.

Non-Profit

Non-profits can play a supplemental role in the development of an informal settlement. There are a large number of non-profits and volunteer groups that come in and out of Botocan. Some of this work has been great but others are not so helpful. The most beneficial have been those organizations that have a permanent presence in Botocan such as the churches in the area. Those groups that just show up with a vanload of free food or clothing are the least helpful.

The non-profits that have really been committed to Botocan have had a positive impact on the community. The churches in the area have seen people's lives transformed. The largest impact by the churches has been among the youth. Many have overcome various addictions and have been able to find employment or attend college.

The presence of churches in the neighborhood provides a source of hope even among those who are not involved. Neighbors and family members have expressed their appreciation of the work that the churches are doing even if they themselves do not attend.

Living in the Neighborhood

One of the remarkable features of Botocan is the extent to which those who serve the neighborhood also live there. My immediate neighbor is one of seven elected community officials. Everyone hired by the government including the local officials, security guards and the ones who sweep trash every morning all live in the neighborhood.

There are many benefits when those who serve the neighborhood also live there. Government officials are kept accountable when the residents see their lifestyles at home. The highest elected official lives in a very small house. He has to be transparent with how the government is run because neighbors will easily notice if his home starts improving. The local government is also very aware of the needs of the residents. They are not the rich deciding what the poor need. Being from the community and remaining there helps the government to offer services that the residents actually want.

Economically, by having all of the local government employees living in the neighborhood, money designated for the community stays in the community. Those paid for their service also contribute to the internal economy when they spend locally.

The pastors living in Botocan recognize that to effectively lead people on their journey with God they must live among them. This allows them to share the pains and joys of the residents. By being respected spiritual figures in the community, they often provide counseling and are called upon to mediate conflict.

Living in the neighborhood means no one really has office hours. They are available anytime for the local community. When the scheduled priest was unable to make it to officiate a funeral service, neighbors asked a local pastor at 6 am if he could conduct a funeral service at 9 am. If one of the local officials is not in the office, it is customary to be told to go to their home.

Participatory

Participatory or citizen involvement is a vital aspect of community development. When the poor participate in the planning process the community will more likely be shaped around their needs.

The track record of failed projects due to the lack of participation is well known. A community development team leader made the following observation of projects that were not participatory.

> The people were passive recipients of development programs. This resulted in associations or projects that did not respond to the community's needs or problems. Their non-participation in its planning and implementation led to the lack of ownership and accountability for the project. These explained the failure of these interventions even in their initial stages.[65]

As a theory, participatory involvement is accepted although in practice it is difficult. When it comes to citizen involvement, there are two options, pseudo-participatory or authentic participatory.

Pseudo-Participatory

The expectation of participatory involvement by citizens creates a dilemma for politicians, corporations, special interest groups, and development workers who have their own agenda. The result is pseudo-participatory; the situation where residents are claimed to be involved in the decision-making process but in reality they are not. Participatory does not mean the residents are allowed to choose between one of two housing designs. Rather, they must be involved in the planning, design, and implementation of projects in their communities.

Pseudo-participatory involvement is not as easy to spot as one would assume. Politicians are very skilled at manipulating town meetings so they can claim to be participatory when in reality it is just a facade. There are many ways that politicians control meetings. The time and location of the meetings can intentionally hinder certain groups from attending. Advance notice of the meetings can be limited and confusing. Meetings are sometimes nothing more than drawn out announcements that leave no time to challenge the plans. When attendees are given the opportunity to ask questions or make suggestions other games can be played. The politician controlling the meeting can plant people in the audience and intentionally limit the questioning to that pre-selected group. That way the politician can claim to only be doing what his or her constituents want.

A large corporation facing public complaints will send its highly trained community relation specialists to hold "participatory" public discussions where residents are given the chance to raise their concerns. These corporate representatives are polite and friendly. More importantly, they seem to have answers backed by the research from specialists and PhDs to show that the company is really looking out for the best interests of the community. It is very difficult to leave one of those meetings and still feel strongly against the company's actions.

These meetings are pseudo-participatory because simply answering questions is not participatory. It is the corporation studying every possible question and having a rehearsed answer. The answers are based on biased research that has a predetermined agenda.

I attended a public meeting in Manila where a government official explained the government's position regarding plans to demolish an informal settlement. The residents wanted to negotiate a compromise where the community would only be partially demolished, so they would still be left with at least a place to live. The official gave a talk on how the government has been extremely generous to the "squatters" over the years. When it was time for questions, the community's spokesperson tried to ask a follow-up question but the official announced only one question per person. No one else was prepared to talk so the questions were either unclear, or unrelated to the compromise the residents wanted. The official closed the meeting with a long speech on how the demolition was actually for the benefit of the "squatters." The meeting ended in frustration on the part of the residents who were never able to present their plans.

Authentic Participatory

The poor themselves should be the main participants in the design of their community. The whole life of the neighborhood from conception onward needs to have authentic participation. When people are involved in the planning, building, and continual improvement of their community they will not want to move. They will develop neighborhood pride and relational bonds with others who are also passionate about their community.

The residents should be the ones who decide which projects should be prioritized. Projects should not be dictated upon a neighborhood. The laws can be changed to put neighborhoods on the right track. However, the residents must be involved throughout the entire process. Transforming a community is slow and gradual. As change happens, some will immediately see the benefits and want the process to move faster. Others will resist and try to stop the changes.

Participation cannot be limited to town meetings. The most vocal and opinionated person can dominate the discussion but not necessarily represent the views of most people in the community. Not everyone can attend these meetings. The elderly and the poor working multiple jobs or those who do not have transportation are left out.

Botocan's development has been exceptionally participatory. When the original residents moved in, they shared in the creation of the community as each person staked out their land and started to build. By the time the government officially recognized Botocan as a community on June 25, 1975, the residents were already established. The government recognition of the neighborhood opened the door for government services.

Botocan is also participatory because it is easy to approach the local officials in order to express concerns or share ideas. This is possible because all of them live in the community. Issues are quickly brought to the attention of the local officials who have the responsibility to address the concern. Issues such as a broken water pipe or an area of the walkway that always floods can be discussed while walking with the official and pointing the problem out to them. I have had local politicians in my home to discuss community issues. They come over as neighbors who face the same issues we do, not as politicians distant from the on-the-ground issues of the community.

6

Walkability

Sustainable and livable neighborhoods that help the poor overcome poverty need to be walkable. According to downtown specialist Jeff Speck, "a walk has to satisfy four main conditions: it must be useful, safe, comfortable, and interesting."[66] Just as important as the four main conditions are what a community does not have such as massive roads, large yards, driveways, and acres upon acres of parking lots in commercial areas. Each of these makes walking longer and more difficult.

Botocan's Features of Walkability

In terms of walkability, informal settlements and Botocan in particular take walking to a whole new level. The entire design of the community assumes that the residents will walk. To get anywhere within the neighborhood everyone walks. Botocan is walkable not only because it is useful, safe, comfortable, and interesting; but also because the community was built to meet the needs of its residents who do not own cars.

Built for Pedestrians

Without even thinking about it, the residents of Botocan walk to where they are going. Even those few residents who do own cars have to walk within the community. This is because Botocan was built for pedestrians. So much so that my home address does not include a street name. Botocan is divided into seven areas. For our address, we use our house number followed by the area instead of a street name. Communities built for pedestrians are not that radical since the idea of having pedestrian-only districts has already been adopted by some cities.

Streets in pedestrian communities are used for walking and bikes. Therefore, they can be significantly narrower than neighborhoods built for cars. The layout of Botocan's walkways allows for multiple options in terms of which one to take. There are usually several ways to get from one place to another, allowing detours to make a purchase or visit a friend. They are also convenient and safe in the event that one walkway is blocked for some reason.

One road goes through Botocan. It is wide enough for a garbage truck, delivery vehicles, and a small fire truck. Bikes, scooters, tricycles, and most of all pedestrians regularly use the main road. The rest of the community is built entirely for pedestrians. The walkways are too narrow for cars and tricycles, but they work well for pedestrians.

The lack of parking is another key feature of being built for pedestrians. Housing and commercial space is so valuable that almost no households in Botocan use part of their property for parking. The only place to park is in one of the neighboring communities. This is also limited since parking is already tight without adding extra cars from elsewhere.

Walking with Purpose

Most neighborhoods are not very walkable regardless of their claim. Yes, it is possible to physically walk around most neighborhoods, but truly being walkable means being able to walk from point A to point B for a purpose. Walking down the street and back does not mean a neighborhood is walkable regardless of its features that supposedly enhance walkability. Good lighting, nature, protection from cars, and a smooth sidewalk do not mean a whole lot when there is no place to go. Usefulness is important for walkability.

It is great to be able to walk simply for the enjoyment of being active. The problem is most of us do not have that kind of spare time. Whenever I try to schedule in time for exercise I never seem to be able to fit it into my day. When it comes to walking, I do not have to try to squeeze it into my schedule. It happens naturally because walking is the means of getting things done. When people walk with a purpose, they will be active. Gottdiener writes, "One estimate claims that Manhattanites walk several miles a day just by taking care of their necessary tasks."[67]

My day begins with a brief walk to a local bakery where I purchase freshly baked bread for breakfast. For lunch, I walk a few minutes from my house and choose from three different home-based restaurants to buy a hot meal. In the afternoon, I walk five minutes to take a broken electric fan to a man in the neighborhood that fixes electronics. He tells me his nephew will walk the fan to my house when it is fixed. On the way home, I pass by the local open-air market to buy fresh fruits and vegetables and walk four minutes to get back to my house. In the evening, my son has a school project with a very specific supply list. We walk a few minutes to the closest school supply store, but they do not have what we are looking for. We have to walk another minute to reach another school supply store, which has exactly what we need. For dinner, my family decides to eat out so we walk fifteen minutes outside of Botocan and choose from dozens of different restaurants. After eating we return home and briefly walk to a church for a program that evening.

Another important feature in terms of usefulness is the ease of getting to other locations in the city. While it is possible to stay in Botocan to work and shop, the broader area significantly adds to the community's sustainability and livability. The majority of the residents work outside the neighborhood bringing money into the community and contributing to the local economy.

There are numerous forms of public transportation within walking distance. Tricycles for short trips can be accessed from within Botocan. Jeepneys[68] traveling to various places around the city can be accessed in a five-minute walk. A fifteen-minute walk will get you to the nearest light rail station providing quick and efficient travel to destinations in the other end of the city.

The surrounding neighborhoods provide access to healthcare. There are dentists, eye doctors, medical labs, family doctors, specialists, and even a hospital within a fifteen-minute walk. When my son needed lab work for his school enrollment, I walked to three different clinics to find the best price. On a different occasion, a friend's daughter slit her wrist on a piece of glass. In less than two minutes, we were at the entrance of the emergency room with the help of a tricycle driver. Pharmacies are also plentiful and within walking distance.

For grocery shopping beyond what is available in the local open-air market there are four neighborhood grocery stores within a fifteen-minute walk. Cooked food is also readily available. Because we do not have to carry anything home when we eat out, the distance we will walk to eat at a restaurant is further than other stores. Within a twenty-minute walk, we have access to everything from street food to fine dining and everything in between.

One of the city's premier food strips is located one block from Botocan. I can walk to eat Korean barbeque, Mexican soft tacos, Italian pizza, and many other local and international cuisines. We also get to enjoy an annual food festival without having to worry about parking or traffic.

The greatest benefit of the surrounding area for local residents is the potential for jobs. The residents seem to work all around the area. Many are within walking distance to their work saving them both time and money.

Safety

Walking in Botocan is as safe as an urban walk can get because there is zero threat of being injured or killed by a car simply because for the most part there are no cars.[69] The main strip has smooth pavement and there is plenty of lighting from public streetlights and private homes. People are outside all the time and there are security cameras so there is really no danger of being robbed or physically attacked while walking through the community. In the event that safety is a concern neighbors will warn pedestrians to go another way. I have never personally had a bad experience while walking through Botocan. I was told of an incident in which a drunken man stopped a teenage girl when she was walking home from class at night. Other bystanders quickly intervened and she was able to continue on her way home.

Going off the main strip and into the labyrinth of homes and businesses is pedestrian-only. This is not always the easiest walk. The walkways are evenly paved for the most part, but there are places where water collects to form puddles. The lighting varies depending on the location. Some of the walkways are well lit from private homes, but there are dark patches. This improved when the government installed solar streetlights. Another concern is that some of the walkways have low beams from second stories that extend into the walkway. Overall safety issues do not prevent people from walking, but there is room for improvement.

Comfortable

Walking in Botocan is comfortable because of the short distance of many of the walks. Most walks are very short because the housing and businesses are compressed in a small area. Even if it is hot or raining I can still go to someone's home or make a purchase without too much discomfort simply because the walk is so short.

As the community developed over the years, the walkways have been paved. Some walkways even have underground pipes that channel rainwater to prevent flooding. This has been one of the slow developments of the community. Slowly but surely the walkways are improving making for a more comfortable walk.

Interesting

Botocan is well suited for an interesting walk. No one walkway is the same. The homes and shops are all different. The local government sponsored respected graffiti artists to paint the main walkway. Some residents have vertical gardens in front of their homes also adding beauty and interest to a walk.

Botocan is mixed-use which adds diversity to a walk. Jane Jacobs writes, "Diversity of uses, on the other hand, while it is too often handled poorly, does offer the decent possibility of displaying genuine differences of content. Therefore these can become interesting and stimulating differences to the eye, without phoniness, exhibitionism, or laboured novelty."[70]

Another important factor in helping to make walking interesting and enjoyable is the friendliness of most neighbors. Houses form the boundaries of the walkways making it easy to talk to neighbors in their doorway or from their windows. The neighborhood has been compared to a college dorm where everyone lives in close contact with each other and is generally friendly. The built environment can help people to treat each other better, which leads to friendlier interactions.

Benefits of Walkability

Walkable neighborhoods are increasingly gaining popularity as more and more people recognize their benefits. These neighborhoods contribute to the health and safety of the residents. They are economical and help small businesses succeed. Walkable neighborhoods also help residents meet each other and are more inclusive. Each of these benefits contributes to the overall wellbeing of the residents.

Health

Walking every day is an important part of physical fitness because it gives the whole body a workout. It is a great way to lose weight by burning excess calories. Walking is a good cardiovascular exercise that helps to lower blood pressure and reduce the risk of heart disease and stroke. Walking is also good for the bones and joints reducing the risk of knee problems and osteoarthritis.

Journalist Charles Montgomery looks at the negative effects of not walking enough. He writes, "Stop moving long enough, and your muscles will atrophy. Bones will weaken. Blood will clot. You will find it harder to concentrate and solve problems. Immobility is not merely a state closer to death: it hastens it."[71] The human body needs to be active in order to be healthy.

Walking in a neighborhood contributes to emotional health. It can be a way to help cope with stress by taking our thoughts away from our problems as we focus on the environment around us. Walking can help physically tire the body so we can sleep better instead of lying awake allowing our mind to become overwhelmed with our anxieties.

Walking can be greatly encouraged by neighborhood design. Speck writes, "Increasingly, it is becoming clear that the American healthcare crisis is largely an urban-design crisis, with walkability at the heart of the cure."[72] A community that is walkable allows its residents to reap the benefits of an active lifestyle.

Safety

Neighborhoods that are walkable are safe. This is because there are many people out on the street or in their homes watching what's going on outside. Common sense tells us "a well-used city street is apt to be a safe street. A deserted city street is apt to be unsafe."[73]

The more walkable a community is the more people will be outside. When people are outside there are many eyes watching the neighborhood. We have had several close calls with small fires that were caught early and put out because people were outside. Children can safely play outside because many people can see them. My elementary age son runs around with his friends. To find them I simply walk to the basketball court near our home and ask neighbors where they are.

Walking to school, work, or to shop greatly reduces the amount of trips taken and the distance traveled in cars. This in return reduces the risk of traffic related injuries and death. A neighborhood built for pedestrians also reduces the risk of automobile related injuries to pedestrians and bikers.

Economical

Walking to shop is a simple way to save money. The cost of gas increases the actual cost of a shopping trip. Even short trips to stores can cost a few dollars in gas. The ability to shop for a wide variety of goods without having to drive helps the poor to stretch their paychecks just a little further.

When neighborhood design assumes people walk instead of drive, public money and land no longer have to be consumed by road construction and maintenance. Public funds would be freed up for other purposes such as increased budgets for schools, health care services, and assistance for small businesses. All of these benefit the broader community and help the poor overcome poverty.

In the United States, if the poor lived in walkable neighborhoods they would no longer have to own a car. The money these families save would be more than they are qualified to receive in the form of government assistance. Instead of forcing the poor to buy cars and then providing food and rent subsidies, neighborhoods should be designed for cars to be a luxury not a necessity.

Botocan serves as a model of a community not designed around car ownership. I only know a few families in Botocan who own a car, and they took on massive debt to do so. Car ownership is a status symbol of the middle class so those families made the choice not because they need a car to get somewhere, but to no longer feel poor.

Enables Small Businesses to Compete with Large Corporations

Small, locally owned businesses are beneficial to the local economy because they tend to offer local products and profits are kept local. Large corporations buy in bulk for all of their stores so they will import products from anywhere in the world as long as it is cheap. It does not matter if the same thing is grown or manufactured where a specific store is located.

Small businesses are able to flourish in walkable neighborhoods. When neighborhood residents walk to do their shopping, they will stay local even if they have to pay more. Residents shop local for numerous reasons. The local stores are very convenient and can be accessed by a short walk. The shop owner is a neighbor so the commercial exchange is also a chance to chat with a friend. Local shops can cater to the specific needs of the community such as selling in very small quantities. The poor do not have extra savings to purchase in bulk nor do they have the storage space to keep it.

Connection to a Neighborhood

Neighborhood design determines how someone is able to get around. Driving and walking create two entirely different perspectives on a neighborhood. Driving shrinks the distance allowing us to barely notice the details of a community. Cars provide a protective bubble with temperature control and sound proofing that hinders the ability to get a true feel for a neighborhood.

Driving causes everyone else to become an object in the way. Other cars just cause traffic. The kids playing on the sidewalk might run out in the street. The old woman with her walker takes a painfully long time to cross the street. The teenagers hanging out on the corner look suspicious and are probably carjackers.

Walking the same neighborhood is a very different experience. There is no sitting blissfully ignoring the sights and sounds of the community. The people outside are no longer threats that will just slow you down, but opportunities to connect with neighbors.

Walking provides a great opportunity to meet people. Walking around Botocan I have been able to meet many of my neighbors. Buying vegetables might take a few extra minutes because I stop to talk with someone along the way.[74]

Inclusive Neighborhoods

Walkable neighborhoods are all inclusive. Bogota's ex-Mayor Enrique Penalosa said, "We need to walk, just as birds need to fly. We need to be around other people. We need beauty. We need contact with nature. And most of all, we need not to be excluded. We need to feel some sort of equality."[75] Walkable communities meet these basic human needs. They are places that can be mixed-income because the poor do not have to buy cars and the emerging middle class knows that walkable neighborhoods are good places to live. The elderly who no longer drive are welcomed since they can safely walk to stores and restaurants. Children and youth can get to places without having to rely on their parents for a ride. The physically handicapped can become more independent since they too can safely travel outside without the fear of cars.

Part III

How Informal Settlements Help the Poor Overcome Poverty and Improve their Lives

The following section examines the design features of communities that help the poor overcome poverty. The poor build communities to meet their needs. As needs change, the communities are adjusted to meet those needs. As the lives of the poor improve, so does their community. Across the globe informal settlements are improving. "Latin American squatter settlements (and illegal subdivisions) have a well-documented history of dynamic change and improvement, which is paralleled, though to a lesser degree, in the rest of the Third World, notably India."[76]

Allen's life today is much different than when he was a child. Growing up in Botocan, Allen experienced the hardships of poverty. In his twenties, he was able to attend college because he was awarded a scholarship through his church. This was directly connected to the relationships he had in church. Another important factor is that Botocan is located within walking distance to a light-rail station. This allowed him to live at home while attending classes. Upon graduation he was offered a high-paying professional job that has greatly improved his family's situation.[77]

Informal settlements help the poor overcome poverty through providing affordable housing, a source of income, and immediate access to goods and services. The community design also helps to foster relationship and adds to the overall quality of life for the residents. These two areas will be examined in this section.

7

From Isolation to Relationships

Humankind is not designed to live in isolation. We are social beings. Relationships are important for our wellbeing. In order to live life to the fullest, we must do it with others.

Neighborhood design determines one's social life. Montgomery writes, "People who live in monofunctional, car-dependent neighborhoods outside of urban centers are much less trusting of other people than people who live in walkable neighborhoods where housing is mixed with shops, services, and places to work. They are also much less likely to know their neighbors."[78] Many people struggle with loneliness because neighborhood design is not concerned with neighbors interacting.

The community we live in can isolate us or help us to socialize. Loneliness is one of the tragedies of failed neighborhood models. The social aspect of human nature has been omitted. People are expected to eat and sleep inside their home and leave their community for everything else. Korten writes, "The modern urban home has become little more than a place to sleep and watch television. Few people find time to participate in the vast array of community activities and services that once made neighborhoods more than a physical address."[79] We have become a society so busy working to pay for mortgages and car payments that by the time we get home after sitting in traffic there is no energy left for socializing.

The whole neighborhood might be neat and organized, but it is also monotonous. The houses look the same since everything is standardized and predictable. The streets have been designed so that if a neighboring site is developed, the communities will not be connected. Zoning laws ensure that no one tries to open a business from their home. The side effect of this type of neighborhood design is there are almost no opportunities to naturally meet neighbors.

Loneliness can greatly diminish one's quality of life. Renowned author Henri Nouwen writes, "Psychiatrists and clinical psychologists speak about it as the most frequently expressed complaint and the root not only of an increasing number of suicides but also of alcoholism, drug use, different psychosomatic symptoms—such as, headaches, stomach and low-back pains—and of a large number of traffic accidents."[80] Neighborhoods that ignore the need for social interaction harm their residents regardless of how ideal and pristine it might look.

Neighborhoods that are designed to foster social interaction help residents move from isolation to relationships. The combination of walkability, mixed-use, and public space all contribute to our ability to socialize within our community. Everyone regardless of social class can have a higher quality of life because of these neighborhood features.

I was walking home from a trip to the playground with my elementary aged son and some of his friends. When we were about a block away from our neighborhood, we passed three guys sitting on the curb. As we approached the entrance to my community, which is a narrow walkway just wide enough for two people to walk through, the other children ran ahead of us and all of a sudden the three guys were there again. This time two of them were blocking the entrance and another one was behind me. I knew it was a bad situation so I grabbed my son and held him. At that point, someone started yelling and everyone looked in our direction. I took the opportunity to make a break for it. When I reached my front door, the children had already told my wife what happened. The man who yelled was the father of one of the children who came to the playground with us. It did not take long for a community leader to visit asking if I wanted to press charges.

I was well protected by my neighbors who risked their own safety to come to my aid. In most cases when someone is being mugged, bystanders do nothing. They are afraid to get involved. Yet, in my case, because my neighbors know me and value our relationship, they intervened.

The social capital of the poor is well accepted. It can "be characterized as a relational construct—a conceptual frame of reference which, even if it is not verbalized by the slum dwellers unless pressed for explanations of their actions, serves as an outline in defining sets of relationships that are vital to the functioning of the community as a whole."[81] The social networks of the poor paint a picture of beauty and resilience in communities not oppressed by failed design or exploitative laws.

Relationships in Informal Settlements

Being a Neighbor

In informal settlements, neighbors are everywhere. Therefore, the residents have to know how to live with each other. Even drug dealers know how to treat others decently. I have talked to people who live near drug houses and the comment is often, "They are nice; I just do not like what they are doing."

Anthropologist Landa Jocano writes of Manila's informal settlers living interdependently with neighbors.

> Neighbors are expected to help one another in times of great need or even in ordinary chores which require the assistance of another person. But such expectations are ingrained in the relationship only when both parties perceive each other as friends. It is common, in this respect, to hear someone call for the neighbor to 'please watch our house while we are away.'

This request later generates reciprocal relations and cements
the interpersonal or inter-familial interactions between those
who are involved.[82]

The residents of informal settlements do not have to fear strangers
because neighbors are all around. The tragic shooting of Renisha McBride
when she knocked on the door of a suburban home in the middle of the
night as she sought help after a car accident would never happen in a high
density informal settlement because neighbors would have helped her.

A group of American students whom I was hosting in Manila had an
evening visitation by a cockroach. They screamed when it started to fly.
Within seconds, they heard a knock at the door and someone asking if
everything was all right. A neighbor heard the screams and went to see if it
was an emergency. They all laughed together when they explained it was just
a cockroach. They also learned that if something did actually happen, help
would soon arrive.

Most people living in informal settlements deserve honorary doctorate
degrees in relationships. They know how to live in a high-density
environment where society's outcasts are forced to live. They also know how
to live with neighbors all around them especially when their neighbors lack
the same civility.

The neighbor that lives right across from me can be challenging at times.
We are separated by a walkway not a road so I can actually stand in my
doorway and touch his wall. He is fine when he is sober, but when he is
drunk he wants to fight. The problem is by the time he comes home well
after midnight no one is around. He just stands outside and yells looking for
someone to challenge him. As one would expect, it is a very unpleasant
experience to be awoken by shouts looking for a fight. Thankfully that only
happens every once in a while, and all of my other neighbors are quiet.

Having a loud neighbor is not unique to Botocan. There can be loud
neighbors anywhere. What makes Botocan special is how others handle the

situation. During one rant on an early Sunday morning, I heard another neighbor step outside and start a friendly conversation with him. The shouting stopped as they sat outside along the walkway and talked over breakfast.

I was so surprised by what had happened I asked the man how he knew to eat breakfast with our drunken neighbor. He replied, "We've known each other for years. He would not fight me. The threats are just a show. All he really wants is someone to talk to. When I realized I was not going to fall back to sleep I decided I better go talk to him so he stops yelling."

Friends and Family

Informal settlements are the home to families. These are mostly honest households where the breadwinner works long days to support their family. Other family members contribute in different ways such as cooking, cleaning, childcare, and managing a home-based store. There is a strong sense of unity within the family.

The family unit goes beyond the traditional nuclear family. For many residents their neighbors are also their extended family. Grandparents, aunts, uncles, and cousins can all live in the same area. Issues do arise when extended families all live in the same small house. That is directly connected to poverty, which causes overcrowding. When each nuclear family has their own separate living space, healthy family relationships can arise.

Most friendships in informal settlements are within the neighborhood. Many people spend the bulk of their free time in the community. Their social circles are their neighbors.

An informal settlement for its residents is a place of friends and family. It is where they want to be because of the relational ties. Being surrounded by friends and family is an important contributor to why people can live in seemingly destitute situations and still enjoy life.

From Self-Reliance to Community-Reliance

American individualism is the culture of self-reliance. Needs are not supposed to be revealed. Social pressure stresses that you are supposed to make it on your own, and your neighbors are supposed to make it on their own.

Informal settlements foster relationships of community reliance. Soliciting donations from neighbors to help fund community events is common. Different organizations will request a letter from the local government giving them authorization to go door-to-door asking for donations for activities such as a basketball league or children's event. The idea is that everyone contributes a very small amount, not one large donor that sponsors the whole activity.

Household tragedies are helped communally. Before leaving for work, Mr. Jenga grabbed his hat stating that he was cold. Being a warm day his family thought it was a strange comment, but did not think much of it. Later that day Mr. Jenga collapsed and died at work. He was the breadwinner of the family. In an instant, a stable household was on the brink of destitute poverty without a source of income, and funeral expenses on top of everything else. Mr. Jenga's son was active in a local church and the congregation came together to help the family. The family was supported emotionally and the financial assistance helped them stay out of debt.

How Informal Settlements Foster Relationships

Neighborhoods with Hope

Hope is cultivated both in the design of the community, and in the process by which it is developed. Botocan is a neighborhood of hope. Therefore, residents regularly take steps to improve their lives and community. They have seen the neighborhood grow and improve, and many have participated in the process. That momentum will continue unless oppressive regulations destroy the process.

Two areas stand out as signs of hope in Botocan, home improvement projects and college attendance. There is usually some form of home improvement projects happening somewhere in the community. Families are investing in their home to make it more comfortable, or they plan to set up a business. Both are positive for the community.

The hopefulness is also seen in the number of young adults studying in college. Families are cutting costs so they can afford tuition payments. There is hope for the future as many realize that education opens doors to good paying jobs.

The hope of the residents helps to build the relational bonds. Hopeful people are friendly and joyful. They are also engaged in their community. Those who are active in their neighborhoods know they cannot do it alone and want others to join them. They are continually spending time with others in the neighborhood so they are able to build friendships with their neighbors.

Houses that Allow Communication with Neighbors

The houses in Botocan are built in ways that help foster relationships. There is no space between homes and the walkways. When I leave my front door open, I can talk with everyone who walks past my house. It is really up to me when and how often I leave the door open. If I am in the mood to talk, I just open the door and chat with people walking by. If I am feeling tired and simply want my personal space, I keep the door shut.

The houses being along the walkway allows for conversations at normal volumes. I do not have to shout and wave at someone walking by because we are not separated by a yard. I can actually be inside my house and have a conversation with people who walk by. Most are just hellos, or other short greetings. However, every once in a while someone will stop and talk for a few minutes.

Many houses are built with large windows facing the walkways. These allow for easy communication with neighbors and are very convenient for opening home-based stores. Windows provide a way to connect with neighbors, but they can also easily be closed for privacy when desired. It is common to walk by someone's home and say a friendly greeting while they are still inside their home.

Heavily Used Public Space

The high population density of Botocan provides the opportunity for constant human interaction in the natural course of life. Simply walking through the community as I go about my day allows me to become familiar with others. We know each other's faces so when we end up buying something from the same store it is not awkward to start a conversation.

Random opportunities to build relationships are magnified in communities with heavily used community space. Because everyone walks, neighbors are often outside creating the natural environment for relationship to be built. It is possible to meet people while walking because there are always opportunities to stop and chat.

Public space in Botocan is heavily used because different people are there for different reasons. The basketball court is really just that, a paved area with a backboard and rim at each end. However, the buildings surrounding the court offer a wide variety of products and services giving a lot of residents different reasons to go there throughout the day. The basketball court is such a popular place to hang out that when you are looking for someone, it is one of the first places to check.

The street life at the basketball court can almost be described as a street party every night. On any given evening there are kids playing tag, teenagers hanging out, and groups of friends chatting. All the while people are regularly passing through as they return from work or school.

The public space is where residents can have shared experiences that help strengthen relational bonds. They stand united as they cheer on neighbors in dance contests, or root for their favorite team in the annual basketball league. So many events take place at the basketball court making it a heavily used public space that helps foster friendships.

Shopping Local

Shopping local in Botocan means buying freshly made bread from Evelyn's bakery. After placing the order we chat for a moment while waiting for Mario, one of the employees, to get the order ready. On the way home, I stop by David's home-based store to pick up some eggs. He does not have change so he tells me he will stop by my house on his way out later in the morning. At the open-air market, I buy vegetables from Shenas who also lives a few houses down from me on the same walkway. She asks what we are going to cook, and updates me on how her family is doing. In the late afternoon, Aling Nena sets up her snack stand at the corner of the basketball court. I ask the children passing my home what she's selling that day. After buying cut pieces of pineapple from Aling Nena, I walk to Nancy's house to place an order for barbeque. On the way home, I literally take about ten steps from Nancy's barbeque to Ajie's burger stall to chat and buy French fries.

The wide range of services available also provides the opportunity to build friendships. The sole of my shoes came loose so I decided to have it sewed instead of buying a new pair. I had noticed that a man had a sign on his door advertising shoe repair. I walked to his place and we negotiated a price. I had never met him before, but now that we had a business exchange I know that his name is Raymond and where to find him if I need his services again. Shopping local means meeting a neighbor and chatting with them while exchanging goods and services.

It is possible to become familiar with the cashiers and clerks when living in a residential only community and driving to a strip mall to grocery shop. How much more meaningful could that relationship be if they were not only someone you knew from shopping, but they also lived near you? Shopping local takes the casual interaction of the transaction and turns it into a real opportunity for a friendship because it is more than business.

Everyone is Welcome

The Bible presents an interesting image of an ideal city. "Once again old men and women will walk Jerusalem's streets with their canes and will sit together in the city squares. And the streets of the city will be filled with boys and girls at play."[83] The elderly sitting together and children playing in the streets is natural in an informal settlement, not a luxury subdivision. Walkable, mixed-use neighborhoods are the best option for there to be lifetime residents. Children, youth, people with disabilities, and the elderly can maintain a high quality of life in such a community.

For many of the residents, Botocan is their home and they have no plans of moving. The homeownership rate of 84% is one indicator of this. More importantly, many of the residents have no desire to live anywhere else. They have invested in their neighborhood and perceive it as the future home of their children and grandchildren. Not because they are destined to live in poverty, but because it is their community. It is where their friends and family live and they have no plans on moving regardless of their job or income level.

Of course, there are people who want to move out, particularly those who are not originally from Botocan. They live there because of the location and affordable rent or their spouse is from Botocan. Some people do eventually immigrate overseas or move somewhere else in the city. For those that choose to move into middle-class housing the community has served its purpose for that family and gave them a chance to get a footing and overcome poverty.

Lifetime residency creates a mentality of intentionally seeking friendships. When someone assumes they will remain in the same location for life, they are motivated to become friends with those around them. Having a good relationship with neighbors is a prioritized value. When neighbors argue, eventually they have to reconcile. You cannot just wait until they move and hope that you get along better with the next set of neighbors.

Lifetime communities need to work for residents of all ages. Starting with birth there needs to be hospitals and pediatricians within a reasonable distance from the community. The community needs to be child friendly providing outdoor space and playgrounds for children to play and accessible high quality education. Youth need fields to play sports and safe places to hangout. They also need opportunities to explore their interests. Adults need meaningful employment and housing security. Seniors need to be able to walk to stores and live in close proximity to medical care.

Botocan is compatible for all by offering something for everyone. Children can play in the walkways and the elderly can sit while talking with friends. People of all ages call Botocan home.

The community also works for those with disabilities. There are a few people with disabilities in Botocan including those who are blind, deaf, and in wheelchairs. Some of the walkways are not wheelchair accessible simply because they are too narrow. The major advantage for people with disabilities in Botocan is the population density and its walkability. The distance needed to travel is minimal, and there are always extra hands willing to help if needed.

During a fire, several men in the neighborhood joined forces to help carry an elderly man in a wheelchair out of his house to safety. That man survived the fire without any injuries because he lived in a high-density informal settlement.

A community with lifetime residents is one in which people have a vested interest in the welfare of the neighborhood. The community enhances the lives of the residents by offering neighborhood features based on the needs of the residents. They are able to live fulfilling lives with meaningful relationships, partly because the community's design encourages neighbors to interact.

8

Quality of Life

It is highly ironic that a beautiful home in an exclusive subdivision can have miserable residents, while the poor whose homes are considered to be uninhabitable can be joyful. This is one of the paradoxes of the modern world.

The design of a community plays a role in helping residents enjoy life. The positive features of informal settlements include walkability, mixed-use, mixed-income, healthy population density, public, private, and non-profit involvement, and environmental sustainability. All of these add to quality of life.

Botocan is a true mixed-income community so there are people in varying degrees of poverty as well as the middle class. Poverty undercuts quality of life in a wide variety of ways including the lack of health care, employment, and educational opportunities. The neighborhood design is able to counterbalance some of the negative effects of poverty, but for some it is not enough. Poverty's grip is too strong. Others are able to overcome poverty, in part because of the design of their community.

Neighborhood Solidarity

Neighborhood solidarity enhances the quality of life for the residents of Botocan. There is a bond among the residents. Being from the same community is itself a point of connection.

The residents help each other. No one will starve to death in Botocan because neighbors will share their extra food if someone is that destitute. The residents have formed an informal community insurance policy. There are no contracts, just the connection as neighbors. When someone needs help the people around them contribute a small amount of the total needed. Eventually the time might come when the roles reverse and the person who gave last year will become the recipient.

Overall there is trust within the community. People leave their door open and are very welcoming. I even know two families who never lock their door. They both own a laptop and other valuables, but have never felt the need to buy a lock. These families live in the heart of an informal settlement whose neighboring middle-class community has fences and multiple locks on their doors because of the supposed criminals in the slum.

One of the reasons for the sense of trust is because people know who is untrustworthy. Neighbors know the ones who are professional thieves and those who are potentially dangerous. It does not take long to learn who cannot be trusted.

The neighborhood solidarity is the result of the mixed-use, walkable design. This allows neighbors to really know each other because there are many opportunities to see each other. Neighbors can be genuine with each other opening the doors for friendship and bonding.

Resilience

The urban poor in general are resilient. They are able to enjoy life as they face hardships. Many are quick to bounce back without anger or bitterness.

Botocan offers two features that contribute to the resilience of the residents. These are employment and recreation options. There are options to earn money through self-employment providing some freedom from oppressive employment laws and exploitative business practices. Recreation options provide a way to relieve stress, remain active, and socialize with friends.

Self-employment options and recreational activities are not simply "bread and circus." That is food and entertainment used to numb the pain of oppression as a way to maintain the status quo. Being self-employed is true empowerment and recreational options help to build community, both of which undercut the system of oppression.

Self-employment is an option for anyone who has space to open a store. The lack of government red tape required to open a home-based business allows families the freedom to open and close stores as needed. When the formal economic system fails to provide enough jobs, the urban poor create their own source of income.

A good laugh with friends is a great stress reliever. This is one of the roles of recreation in a community. The entertainment options in Botocan are inexpensive and accessible. Sports events are common. Basketball and volleyball are the most popular and can be played almost anytime. There are pool tables and darts operated by private citizens, and sometimes table tennis is set up on the stage at the main basketball court.

Physical Activity

Health is an important part of quality of life. A neighborhood can contribute to health by being walkable and having various options for physical activity. In this respect, Botocan is built for physical activity. Being a walkable neighborhood, every resident must do some walking even if it is short distances.

The high population density allows for a variety of fitness opportunities. During the summer, there are various organized fitness groups such as weekly Zumba and exercise sessions for the elderly. Athletic organizations are also popular such as basketball leagues and a biking club. The basketball courts makes physical activity possible by providing the public space needed for athletic activities. During the development of the community, residents made the decision that no one would be allowed to build in certain areas to make room for basketball courts.

Cultural Expression

Cultural expression helps to enrich neighborhood life. Community sponsored cultural events are regular occurrences in Botocan. These events are entertaining and provide the opportunity for neighbors to enjoy shared experiences. For the participants they provide a venue to showcase their talents and learn important life skills such as performing under pressure. The youth in the community are able to become involved in enriching activities that are the stepping-stones for future achievements.

There are so many different cultural events held throughout the year that almost everyone can find something of interest. The most popular are the summer basketball league and the local fiesta. Other common activities are singing and synchronized dancing. On occasion, there are other events. I have seen everything from boxing to ballet.

Cultural expression includes celebrations. Neighborhood celebrations allow people to enjoy life together. The local fiesta is a major annual celebration. The preparations start several weeks before the fiesta. On the day of the fiesta, the neighborhood is lively from sunrise until late in the night. The event itself acts to create social bonds as people spend time enjoying life together.

The design of Botocan contributes to cultural expression because it is a walkable, high-density community with a central public space and multipurpose streets. The residents can easily come and go to different events as they please without having to worry about parking or having to stand all day.

Faith

Quality of life is enhanced by the sense of purpose and meaning found in deep religious faith. The three major churches in Botocan: Faith Gospel Community, Botocan Bible Christian Fellowship, and a Catholic chapel are all seeing lives transformed because of faith. One man's grandmother described him as being passed out drunk for years before he started attending church. He has now been sober for several years. Another man worked as a thief robbing people at gunpoint until he realized he could not maintain that lifestyle forever. He became involved in church and started working legitimate jobs.

The churches have their buildings within Botocan. From the outside, they blend in with the surrounding homes. They are within walking distance for all of the members so they truly function as community churches. The church buildings also serve as a sanctuary for those seeking shelter. After a fire the churches functioned as temporary relief centers. The churches also open their doors for young women seeking a safe place to sleep because men are drinking in their home.

Safety

Botocan is a safe neighborhood. The population density ensures a level of safety from violent crimes. Arguments are usually quelled before they get out of hand, because the security guards are called when neighbors hear shouting. Domestic violence cannot be hidden because neighbors can hear shouting from within other homes. There is violence and abuse but the social pressure from knowing that neighbors can hear and the professionalism of the local security force helps to limit it.

One might assume that the high population density of an informal settlement is a breeding ground for disease. This does not have to be the case. The most common health related concerns among children are head lice and pinkeye. These are minor and easily treated. The major sicknesses that are dangerous are dengue fever and tuberculosis. Mosquitoes cause many deadly diseases and are combated by removing all possible breeding grounds. Tuberculosis is an airborne disease that is aggressively addressed by the public health department in order to prevent its spread.

Personal Growth

The ability to grow as a person adds to quality of life. Personal growth expands one's perceptions and opportunities. It helps people to get involved in neighborhood issues and contributes to the improvement of the whole community.

The neighborhood design helps contribute to personal growth. The residents are full participants in the design and construction of the community. The residents determine what their homes look like and what they are used for. They are able to adjust their home to best meet their changing needs.

There are plenty of opportunities for personal growth within Botocan. The local government offers a variety of seminars for anyone in the community. Some examples include technical skills trainings and classes for the high school equivalency exam.

Botocan has several organizations such as churches and social clubs that provide leadership opportunities for local residents. Local churches regularly conduct leadership training and help many people develop their leadership abilities. Amor is a great example. As a teenager, she started attending church. The pastor's family cared for her and helped her finish high school. Church members also connected Amor to a woman who helped raise a full scholarship so Amor could attend college. She graduated college and currently works in a prestigious government job. Amor was also elected to serve in the local government.[84]

Part IV

How the Entire City Benefits from Informal Settlements

Communities across the economic spectrum can all benefit from the ingenuity of how the poor build their neighborhoods.[85] These communities have the potential to free up public land that would otherwise be used for roads. Traffic and air quality will improve as more people move into pedestrian prioritized communities. Even those in rural areas can benefit, as more land will be available for farms and forests that can be enjoyed by all.

Informal settlements can serve as a model of sustainable development. Designing neighborhoods based on how the poor build their communities can help provide a path out of poverty. They will also help everyone else in the surrounding area by improving the quality of life for all by adding to the vibrancy of an area and contributing to environmental sustainability.

9

Healthy Cities

Healthy cities are livable and sustainable. They are places where those with resources can enjoy the best a city has to offer and where the poor are not marginalized and are able to improve their lives. Informal settlements contribute to the overall health of a city by adding to its vibrancy, ensuring cost effective services, reducing homelessness, and providing a real solution to traffic.

A Vibrant Community

A vibrant community adds to quality of life. Vibrancy brings a sense of joy and excitement as people interact for business and leisure. It is the city at its best. The street life of a city is a quick way to determine its health. Jane Jacobs states it well, "there exists no substitute for lively streets."[86] Lively streets are where informal settlements excel.

The features of a vibrant community include a variety of things to do and an accessible public transit system. It is an area that is full of life and activities from a diverse group of users who are there for different reasons. Gottdiener writes, "Lively street scenes filled with pedestrians at all hours not only deter crime, but it is the very hallmark of a healthy city."[87]

Vibrancy is dependent on work and leisure activities being integrated into neighborhoods. It is impossible to have a vibrant neighborhood in a single-use location. Even popular shopping districts that are sometimes full of people only give a façade of vibrancy because they lack diversity since people are there for limited reasons.

While vibrant neighborhoods are mixed-use, they are still heavily residential. They therefore provide housing that enables the high-density needed for vibrancy. Informal settlements have an abundant stock of housing, which allows them to be good for businesses. They provide both workers and customers for shops.

Vibrancy is felt in the number of people on the street. I can walk outside and easily see dozens of people hanging out. The residents make use of public space and local shops. This is what makes informal settlements vibrant places.

Cost Effective Services

Walkable, mixed-use, mixed-income communities with healthy population densities are cost effective. They allow for efficiency of government programs and the distribution of goods and services. If the 8,000 people living on 20 acres in Botocan were spread out in typical suburban sprawl with single-family homes on quarter acre lots, roads, parking lots, and a separate commercial district with an average of six people per acre the results would be disastrous.[88] This would create massive sprawl consuming about 1,333 acres or about 2 square miles of land.

Maintaining the road network and government services needed for a 2 square mile neighborhood is significantly more costly than servicing a community on 20 acres. In her book, *The End of the Suburbs*, Leigh Gallagher writes:

> Sprawling development is more expensive to build. Roads are wider and require more paving. Water and sewage service costs are higher. It costs more to maintain emergency services since more fire stations and police stations are needed per capita to keep response time down. Children need to be bused farther distances to school.[89]

The government is exempt from this extra expense in informal settlements because of their walkable, high-density design. These communities allow for cost effective government services such as mail delivery, police patrols, fire departments, and public schools. High-density allows mail delivery to be in one location instead of each individual house. Police patrols can be done on foot freeing police departments from needing to provide every officer with an expensive vehicle. Schools that are in areas where the entire student body walks do not have the extra expense of operating buses.

The cost of government services reduces in proportion to an increase in population density. The hidden subsidies for low-density communities are the extra costs needed to service these neighborhoods. "The most sprawled-out American cities spend an average of $750 on infrastructure per person each year."[90] The inefficiencies of sprawl are costly. Montgomery writes, "Not only does sprawl development cost taxpayers more to build, it costs more to maintain, because each home in a typical community of dispersed single-family homes on big lots needs so much more paved street, drainage, water, sewage, and other services than a home in a denser, more walkable place."[91] Low-density neighborhoods drain public funds.

It is interesting that those who are against welfare for the poor are often the very ones who receive even more welfare without realizing it. When presenting a public lecture on reimagining slums I was asked about justice for the middle class. This question assumes that the poor exploit the rich. The reality is that the middle and upper classes also receive welfare. It is just called government services, not welfare.

Reduce Homelessness

If the poor were persecuted globally for constructing their own homes the way they are in the US, the global rates of homelessness would skyrocket. There would be millions more people sleeping in the streets. The social and public health risks would reach epidemic proportions.

The number of people without a home would be greatly reduced if tent cities in the US were invested in and communities modeled after informal settlements existed in every city in America. Informal settlements ensure that there is enough affordable housing because they allow for houses of all sizes. Neuwirth writes, "Not one government in existence is successfully building for the poorest of the poor. So the poorest of the poor are building for themselves. They may not fit into any great ideological category, and it is certainly illegal according to current law. But it is sensible, patriotic, and worthy of a true citizen."[92]

In the US, the jump from homelessness to renting an apartment is huge. A neighborhood designed to help the poor overcome poverty could offer low-cost rental units for someone coming off the streets. It would also allow someone who has fallen on hard times to downsize to something they can afford so they do not become homeless.

A mixed-use, mixed-income, walkable neighborhood will allow someone to purchase an inexpensive home as a way to eliminate monthly rent. Residents would be motivated to turn their skills into home-based businesses to both increase their income and provide their neighbors with a service.

Some cities are experimenting with tiny homes as a way to reduce homelessness. Even this is an uphill battle because of oppressive zoning regulations and building codes, as well as slumophobic neighbors that care more about their property value than the suffering they cause others.[93] Tiny homes have great potential to help the homeless, but not in the way that tiny home parks for the homeless are currently being implemented. A residential only, tiny home park for the homeless managed by a wealthy outsider is just a repeat of failed public housing projects. It is the same oppressive structure in a different form.

Cities considering tiny homes as a way to reduce homelessness need to take a more holistic approach and fully embrace mixed-use, mixed-income, walkable neighborhoods that are high-density and interconnected with the broader city. When tiny homes are incorporated into a larger effort to help the poor improve their lives, they have great potential to reduce homelessness.

A Real Solution to Traffic

Single-use zoning that places cars at the center of life is the largest contributor to traffic. Instead of enjoying life, people are forced to spend hours in their car each day just to go to work, shop, or visit friends. Jane Jacobs writes, "Lack of wide ranges of concentrated diversity can put people into automobiles for almost all their needs."[94]

There is an obsession with widening existing roads and spending billions on building highways. Yet, traffic still gets worse. Highway building in order to solve traffic is the epitome of the cobra effect. Legend has it; during the colonial era, the British in India had a phobia of the local wildlife, particularly the intimidating and venomous cobras. The colonial government came up with a scheme to get rid of the cobra problem. They would pay for dead cobras. The idea was that if someone caught and killed a cobra they could turn it in for a cash reward. Sounds like a win-win situation for everyone.

Unfortunately for the government, the citizens realized the once worthless cobras were now valuable. Instead of simply capturing and killing the snakes, some people started breeding them. This approach was much more profitable and a whole lot safer than trying to hunt wild cobras. Eventually the colonial leaders realized what was happening and revoked the original ordinance making cobras worthless once again. Now that breeding cobras was no longer profitable, the only sensible thing to do was to release them into the wild. The result of the original program to eliminate the threat of cobras actually increased their population. The cobra effect has become the term used to describe a situation where the intended solution to a problem actually makes it worse.

Highway building and widening are not the solution to traffic problems even though there is nonstop construction in the attempt to reduce traffic. The problem is that road projects add to the number of cars on the street. Transportation expert Samuel Schwartz writes, "The really insane idea, the one we keep trying over and over again with exactly the same crappy results, is fixing congestion by building more roads."[95] The reason for this is induced demand. "Induced demand is the name for what happens when increasing the supply of roadways lowers the time cost of driving, causing more people to drive and obliterating any reductions in congestion."[96]

A conversation I had with a man who supported a road widening project demonstrates this phenomenon. He shared that he rarely drives to that end of town because of traffic and claimed, "Once the road is finished I'll be able to drive there more often because it will be faster." His reason for wanting the road project is logical, but also shows why it is bound to cause more traffic. He is planning on driving more often and longer distances because of the convenience provided by the road project. The result is even more cars on the road causing even more traffic.

Journalist Nick Summers explained induced demand in an article addressing traffic in New York City. He Writes:

> In general terms, traffic is caused by too much demand (from vehicles) meeting too little supply (roads). One solution is to increase supply by building more roads. But that's expensive, and demand from drivers tends to quickly overwhelm the new supply; today engineers acknowledge that building new roads usually makes traffic worse. Instead, economists have suggested reducing demand by raising the costs of driving in congested areas.[97]

When evaluating the math, it seems that if you have 100 cars and move them from one lane to three you would only have 33 cars per lane and thus cut traffic by 1/3. The problem is more and wider roads encourage more driving. When there were 100 cars on the one lane road, I might not have taken that extra trip, but now that it is only 33 cars per lane I will. And just like that the 100 cars on the road quickly becomes into 101 and so on. It is not long before the number of cars on the road surpasses the original 100 per lane to the point where traffic is even worse and citizens are demanding that city councilors and county supervisors come up with a solution. The solution is usually more road construction.

Road building is the wrong solution because it looks at the problem of traffic from a flawed perspective. Road building seeks to get people from point A to point B as quickly as possible. This is flawed because aside from tourist destinations, points A and B do not have to be fixed locations. What if points A and B were brought together? What if my home, point A, and a place to buy bread, point B, were within walking distance in a mixed-use community? That would reduce traffic because it would mean less driving trips to the grocery store. Schwartz writes, "What matters is *access*. And it's just as easy, and a lot more efficient, to improve access—to stores, or entertainment, or employment—by decreasing the distance between, for example, home and supermarket than it is by increasing the speed by which to get from one to the other."[98]

The focus on reducing traffic must be on reducing the number of vehicle trips taken per day. According to urban planner Jeff Speck, "The only way to reduce traffic is to reduce roads or increase the cost of using them."[99] For the poor, the cost of driving is already painful. When they are provided with viable alternatives, many people will choose to stay off the roads, thus reducing traffic. Therefore, the alternative to road building as the solution to traffic is mixed-use, mixed-income, and walkable communities. These communities lower the number of trips that people need to make by car. They also lower the percentage of driving residents. This is the only true solution to traffic.

10

Environmental Sustainability

Environmental sustainability is an important consideration in community design. The community that the residents of Botocan have built is environmentally friendly. Some of this has been by default because the poor have to live without consuming vast amounts of energy and resources. The other way that Botocan is environmentally friendly is the design of the community.

Houses come in a variety of sizes because the community is mixed-income. Households can reduce their energy consumption as much as they want without city ordinances or homeowners associations legislating high-energy use in the form of minimum building sizes and forbidding clotheslines.

But Informal Settlements Look Like Environmental Hazards

Large informal settlements are not typically considered environmentally friendly. Visually, the ramshackle houses look more like urban squalor than models of environmental sustainability. Some homes seem to have their junk collection on their roof.[100] There is an overall lack of green space within informal settlements. No one has lawns and trees are scarce.

Some of the households in Botocan still do not have a toilet. In this case, several households will share one. There is no septic or city sewage and all the toilets flush into canals. Most of these are covered but one is exposed and flows like a small creek through the community. The open canal runs right along the side of my house so I know how polluted the water is. There are times when I have showered and wondered if the soap was rotten before quickly realizing that the smell was from the canal. Amazingly, it is not entirely dead. I have seen live earthworms in the water.[101]

The dirty water, lack of plant life, and general grunginess of the community are not the whole picture. The environmental destruction caused by the 8,000 residents of Botocan is felt immediately in the community, but the damage they cause elsewhere is minimal.

The ecological footprint of informal settlements is mainly limited to the immediate area of the community itself. On the other hand, a wealthy community with beautifully manicured lawns and professional landscaping negatively impacts the environment for miles. Their ecological footprint goes far beyond the immediate community. The environmental damage done by high-energy neighborhoods is felt across the globe.

Unlike the upper classes, the poor immediately suffer from their own environmental destruction. Dumping trash in the waterways causes their homes to flood. Burning plastic causes them to choke on horrible smelling fumes. The poor have a felt need for environmental sustainability. Evans writes, "In trying to solve the environmental problems of their own local space, the poor can become agents of more universal interests."[102] In this way, informal settlements can serve as models for environmentally sustainable communities.

Environmentally Friendly Design

The design of the community contributes to being environmentally friendly. As was already discussed in Chapter 6, Botocan was built for pedestrians. Walking is the environmentally friendly way to travel. It helps the environment by eliminating harmful emissions from cars and thereby reducing the amount of greenhouse gases that are released into the atmosphere. The improved air quality in and of itself is a huge benefit to the environment.

The houses themselves are built over a long period of time using both new and used materials. Without restrictive building codes, residents are able to use perfectly good scrap materials that would otherwise end up in landfills.

The residents are allowed to build their homes in ways that meet their need for minimal energy use. Windows can be located where they provide maximum light depending on the angle of their home in relation to the sun. They are not restricted by a unified building code that could care less about maximizing the morning sun. On a sunny day, I do not need to use the lights at all in my home. In fact, when I turn them on it barely makes a difference.

My home has another great energy efficient feature. During the heat of the day, the inside stays cool. Neighbors have come into my house and asked if we have air conditioning because it is much cooler inside. I assumed that it was an accident until I talked to the architect and builder. His years of construction experience taught him that the house would stay cool because of how he built it.

Another important factor is that the businesses are locally owned. Since the business owners live in the neighborhood, they also suffer if they pollute the neighborhood. This is not the case in other neighborhoods where companies could care less about the environmental impact on a community because the owners do not live there.

Slums to Save the Countryside

Imagine the loss for future generations if the beauty of nature from lush green forests and farm fields disappeared. Sadly, the countryside is slowly being destroyed. Sprawl is replacing the natural beauty of farmland and forests.

Cities are often viewed as environmental hazards. This perception ignores the ecological footprint per person. An individual living in a high-density, walkable, mixed-use, mixed-income community has much less ecological footprint than someone living in sprawl.

It is true that high-density areas destroy the local habitat. Therefore, it is easy to falsely conclude that low-density communities are environmentally friendly. This is a grave misunderstanding. Low-density areas also destroy the environment. They might look clean and green, but grass is not a sign of a healthy environment. If anything, grass signifies the use of chemicals from fertilizer, herbicide, and insecticide, which flow into the water supply.

Economist Edward Glaeser's insightful article, *If you Love Nature, Move to the City*, argues for high-density living for environmental reasons. Glaeser writes, "We are a destructive species, and if you love nature, stay away from it. The best means of protecting the environment is to live in the heart of a city."[103] Low-density living is one of the worst environmental choices one can make.

The only way to stop sprawl from destroying the countryside is through high-density, walkable, mixed-use, mixed-income communities. Speck writes, "There are only so many people in the United States at any given time, and they can be encouraged to live where they have the smallest environmental footprint. That place turns out to be the city—the denser the better."[104]

Pseudo to Authentic

I saw a bumper sticker in a suburban town that read, "I care for creatures." The first thing I thought of was how many animals that car killed. I have no doubt that the owner of the car cares about animals and would never intentionally hurt one. But the fact is that cars are a huge hazard for all animals. Just observe the number of dead animals along the road. Cars kill endangered species, pets, and regular wildlife.

The push for environmentally friendly cars and other technological improvements is only a partial solution because it does not address the other hazards of cars. Electric cars might not use gas or give off harmful emissions, but they still do not help the poor, elderly, and the physically disabled who suffer because of the driving culture. Electric cars still kill people not to mention animals and pets. Electric cars get their electricity from somewhere. Even if the electricity comes from solar or wind it is still not perfect.

Professor and author, Witold Rybczynski, concludes that green building design and electric cars are positive but flawed.

> These technological fixes are undoubtedly useful, but they
> conceal a basic truth. Rather than trying to change behavior to
> reduce carbon emissions, politicians and entrepreneurs have
> sold greening to the public as a kind of accessorizing. 'Keep
> doing what you're doing,' is the message, just add a solar panel,
> a wind turbine, a bamboo floor, whatever. But a solar-heated
> house in the suburbs is still a house in the suburbs, and if you
> have to drive to it—even in a Prius—it's hardly green.[105]

Rybczynski makes an important point. Energy efficient cars and building are just accessories. They are important and do make a difference, but not much.

As much as people would like to continue living as carelessly as we always have, there are really no perfect energy options. They all have their problems. Even green energy, which helps us feel less guilty, and therefore encourages more use. This can actually nullify the energy efficient benefits.

One's choice of where they live will determine more than anything else how much of an impact they have on the environment. Anyone serious about environmentalism needs to consider the neighborhood they live in. This is the most important environmental decision we can make. Neighborhood design can make an environmentally friendly lifestyle joyful and natural, or impossible and frustrating. An environmentally friendly neighborhood is walkable, mixed-income, and mixed-use such as informal settlements.

Those with resources have the responsibility to live in environmentally friendly neighborhoods. When people with resources choose to live in mixed-income, mixed-use, walkable communities they create the demand for this type of neighborhood and motivate developers to build them.

Part V

Designing Communities that Help the Poor Overcome Poverty

The world has much to learn from informal settlements. Botocan demonstrates that the poor have developed a sustainable and livable neighborhood that helps the residents overcome poverty. The community meets the needs of the residents while contributing to their quality of life.

Informal settlements are far from perfect. However, their problems are associated with poverty and oppressive policies, not the design of the community. The issues of poverty and oppression cannot be ignored. The solution is to keep the positive features of informal settlements and adopt them into community design while at the same time address the issues of poverty.

The UN has a goal of "improving substantially the lives of at least 100 million slum dwellers, while providing adequate alternatives to new slum formation."[106] This goal is described as, "a twofold challenge: improving the lives of existing slum dwellers and planning adequate alternatives for future urban growth."[107] Both of these objectives can be addressed through adopting the positive features of informal settlements into neighborhood design.

In the last section, I will examine the application of reimagining slums. The emphasis is how to better walk beside the poor in their effort to improve their lives. After examining the legal structure needed for communities to help the poor, I will look at addressing poverty while keeping the positive features of informal settlements. The last chapter briefly examines implementing the lessons learned into community design.

11

Policies We Can All Live By

Most Governments have failed to help the poor overcome poverty. Community organizer Edward Chambers observed, "Nearly fifty years have passed since poverty and urban decay became matters of major attention and contention in America (eliminating slums, LBJ's war on poverty, etc.). But after decades of ideological argument and top-down bureaucratic experimentation, our cities are still drowning in poor people, violence, and desperation."[108] Even the UN recognizes the failure of governments to adequately address poverty. "The most important factor that limits progress in improving housing and living conditions of low-income groups in informal settlements and slums is the lack of genuine political will to address the issue in a fundamentally structured, sustainable and large-scale manner."[109] Politicians must be pressured to reverse oppressive policies and implement ones that help the poor improve their lives.

There is a lot of focus on "smart growth" but there does not seem to be any consensus on what that actually means. What is for certain is that most growth is only smart if you are not low-income. Change needs to happen and the only way to do that is to change policies.

Governmental policies play a huge role in whether or not a community will help the poor improve their lives and overcome poverty. The policies recommended in this chapter are generic and not directed at a specific location. They are intended to get politicians, city planners, and concerned citizens talking about ways they can make neighborhoods work on behalf of the residents and become more sustainable and livable for all.

Policies that improve the lives of the poor and work for greater equality also benefit all of society. Wilkinson and Pickett write, "The evidence shows that reducing inequality is the best way of improving the quality of the social environment, and so the real quality of life, for all of us."[110] Policies that help the poor are not an injustice against the upper classes. In fact, the upper classes also benefit when the poor overcome poverty. "Greater equality brings substantial gains even in the top occupational class and among the richest or best-educated quarter or third of the population, which include the small minority of the seriously rich. In short, whether we look at states or countries, the benefits of greater equality seem to be shared across the vast majority of the population."[111]

Communities need to be designed and built for justice not property values. Neighborhood design based purely on property values will always result in oppression and exploitation. The rich currently shape communities for their benefit. Until this changes, oppressive communities will continue to be the norm.

In order for communities to better serve their residents, zoning laws and building codes need to be revised. This starts with rethinking housing.

Rethinking Housing

A few years ago, my son asked me to draw a house. I am not much of an artist, but a house is something I can certainly draw. At least that is what I thought. I confidently took my paper and pencil and proceeded to draw a square with a triangle as the roof. From there I added a rectangle at the bottom as a door and drew four squares as windows. I was fairly pleased with my generic house. My son on the other hand was not impressed. He informed me, "That's not a house!" I replied, "Yes it is." He started to cry and said, "Please draw a house." I decided to draw our home in an informal settlement. I drew a rectangle with a door and a large window on the left and a small window on the right along with the small canal that runs along the side of our home. He was very happy with this house.

Throughout history, people have lived in many different style homes. Whatever structure served their needs with readily available materials was their home. Native Americans lived in tepees, wigwams, cliff dwellings, igloos, and numerous other housing styles. No anthropologist would describe Native Americans as homeless because they do not consider the structures they lived in proper homes. Imagine the cultural insensitivity and arrogance of telling someone that the homes their ancestors used for centuries are not fit for human habitation and therefore not real houses.

Telling the poor that their home is not really a house and is actually illegal is an attack on the poor and oppressive. Yet, it happens all the time when referring to the homes of the poor. A structure that is someone's place of residence is a house and should be considered as such under the law. A house can be any structure that someone lives in regardless of shape, size, and building material.

A house cannot be limited to single-family homes, townhouses, or apartments. A house is much more than a building. It is a place of security, privacy, and safety. It is a place to keep warm and to sleep without the threat of being awakened by a beating.

Sleeping on the sidewalk is very dangerous. The homeless are murdered, raped, and assaulted when they are asleep and defenseless. Living without a home is significantly worse than in a tiny shanty surrounded by others who also built similar homes.

A house is also a source of empowerment. "I have a house" is a powerful statement. The shame of homelessness is eliminated when you have an address. Laws governing housing need to work to ensure that everyone has a place to call home.

Revising Building Codes

I saw news footage of a storm in the United States while I was in the home of a construction worker in Manila. He commented, "Americans don't know how to build houses. We have storms like that every year but our homes are not destroyed." This comparison was of houses in Manila's informal settlements to homes in an American suburb. According to this man who has built homes for years without using building codes, his work is better and safer than the highly regulated homes of America. I was embarrassed by his comment, but there was no argument that the homes being flattened by a storm were obviously cheaply built.

Botocan was built with self-imposed safety codes. After about fifty years of development, no one has died because a building collapsed. I asked the owner of a three-story structure he built himself if he planned to add a fourth floor. He responded that the foundation was only strong enough for three floors. He did not know the strength of the foundation based on precise calculations. However, after twenty years of construction experience he knew that three stories would be safe. Adding another floor was a risk he was not willing to take.

Building supplies do not come easy for the poor so they are not going to risk the destruction of their home by cutting corners, or expanding beyond what the foundation can support. The homes in Botocan are safe even without bureaucrats dictating the terms of safety.

This does not mean that there are no safety concerns related to the buildings. Strong winds can blow roofs off. Some of the stairs are more like ladders and can be dangerous for children or the elderly. Cheaper building materials are often flammable, so the risk of fire is also a concern.

The reality is that the poor have built the homes that they live in as safely as they can considering the available resources and the freedom to build. The UN Millennium Project Task Force on Improving the Lives of Slum Dwellers recommends that building codes "should reflect the special needs of the urban poor with respect to minimum plot size, incremental construction, and home-based economic activities."[112]

Small inexpensive homes are vital for the poor. The smallest home I have ever seen was 6 foot by 3 foot (18 square feet). The owner had a sleeping mat and a small elevated shelf where he kept his clothes and a few books. He shared a bathroom with his neighbors. His home was certainly tiny but he was not homeless. It was his, he was proud of it, and he fought the government when they eventually destroyed his home for being "unsafe."

There should be no minimum lot and unit size requirements. Someone should be allowed to build as small of a house as they want to live in. Small homes reduce costs beyond the cheaper homeownership and rental costs. They also reduce the cost of utilities and greatly increase the potential for net zero electricity consumption.

The most regulated building code in one area of Botocan is the requirement to not build with cement or steel. The residents must build with wood and other light materials. This results in an unsafe fire hazard legally created by the building code. The viciousness of this oppressive building code was revealed when a fire hit that area of Botocan and the residents were temporarily forbidden from rebuilding because the area was deemed unsafe. The residents followed the building code imposed on them and they ended up losing their homes because of it.

One of the great contradictions of building codes is the effort that goes into making sure the structure is safe from every possible form of freak accident without any thought about the risk the occupants take every day when they have to drive to school, work, and stores. Safety cannot be limited to individual homes. The entire community needs to be taken into consideration. The major safety issue in today's neighborhoods is car accidents. Neighborhoods that require driving to work and shop are safety hazards. The World Health Organization estimates "There were 1.25 million road traffic deaths globally in 2013."[113] According to the National Safety

Council in the United States, there were about 40,100 traffic deaths in 2017.[114] There are millions of traffic related injuries in the US. Forcing residents to drive for every need is a major safety hazard, and yet it is overlooked in building codes.

Traffic engineer Charles Marohn has an insightful article on road design called *Confessions of a Recovering Engineer*. Marohn writes, "Wider, faster, treeless roads not only ruin our public places, they kill people. Taking highway standards and applying them to urban and suburban streets, and even county roads, costs us thousands of lives every year."[115] Marohn confesses that roads are not designed based on the needs and wants of the local residents. He refers to a typical problem in community development when professionals think they know more about how to solve someone's problem than the person themselves. On this Marohn writes, "A fair percentage of my time was spent convincing people that, when it came to their road, I knew more than they did."[116]

Neighborhoods that are built for car ownership not only put the drivers at risk but also endanger those in the community who do not drive. Walking and bike riding are discouraged by the threat of being hit by a car. The elderly who have slower reflexes and may not hear or see very well are at risk of being hit whenever they venture outside. Children are also at risk when they play outside. Even if they have a large yard, if a ball rolls into the street a child will follow it without looking.

The more people have to drive the more they are at risk of a car accident. Building codes need to include the distance from the nearest grocery store and school as one of the safety concerns. This would be one way to encourage mixed-use, walkability, and higher population density.

Building codes that deal with structural safety should be the bare minimum and allow for a variety of building styles and materials. Building codes should work on behalf of the poor and not add to their suffering.

Building codes are needed when a real estate developer builds homes for the sole purpose of making money. In this case, they are meant to protect the public from shady business practices. Homebuilders need to be held accountable for the safety and quality of the houses they build. This is the real value of building codes and in these situations; they need to be in place.

Every neighborhood should not be regulated by the same generic legislation that is designed for a specific situation. There should be different codes for real estate development corporations set on earning maximum profit and those building a home so their family is not homeless. Someone who wants to build a home to live in should not be under the same scrutiny. They are the ones who will live in the house so they should be trusted to build it in a way that meets their needs.

Building codes must address the needs of the poor for flexibility regarding housing. A tent is perfectly safe for anyone around it, and it at least provides a family with a place to sleep. Why not let a family live in a tent and save money to build a more permanent roof to protect them from the rain? After a while, they will be able to make more and more improvements until they have a small one-room home that protects them from the weather and gives them a place to store their possessions. Eventually they might even be able to put in plumbing and other improvements to make life a little more comfortable.

This scenario is not possible under current building codes. Instead of having the dignity of being homeowners, the family will sleep on the sidewalk because "safety codes" do not allow them to live in their home. The children suffer as they are bounced around from shelters, charity organizations, and social services. The family is worse off and more public funding is spent to "serve" them.

No one wants to see someone killed because of faulty design and construction. But that risk needs to be balanced with all the other alternatives. Is it better to live in a shack so that the family has enough money to eat every day and even some extra for emergencies like doctor visits, or live in a home built to code and suffer from chronic hunger and all the health problems caused by malnutrition? This decision needs to be made by the families themselves. Both options should be available. Cities and counties in the United States have already made the decision that a home built to code is better than feeding children. These policies disempower the poor from making very basic decisions that have a major impact on the wellbeing of their families.

The process for obtaining building permits should be streamlined and scaled. Small, one-story structures should not need any permits if it is built and maintained by the owner occupant. The larger the structure and the more potential impact on neighbors and the environment, the more government control there needs to be. This would help the poor avoid costly and time-consuming building permits.

The poor build their homes as they are able to come up with supplies, so projects tend to sit unfinished while they are saving money for the next phase. Building codes for the poor need to acknowledge this fact so they cannot be time bound.

Building codes need to assist homeowners in making home improvements. This requires codes to be clear and available so that homeowners can work on their home without having to hire an expensive contractor. When building codes hinder do-it-yourself home improvements they prevent the poor from working within the legal structure and incentivize illegal construction. In contrast building codes can work for the poor. Safety inspectors should be available to work with homeowners to ensure fire and structural safety. They can serve as coaches by helping people make desired improvements on their homes in ways that are safe, efficient, and meet their needs.

Building codes need to be reviewed so that they are really about safety. Unnecessary codes should be revised or deleted altogether. The review board needs to include the poor, not rich lawyers who have no idea what life is actually like in poverty.

Revising Zoning Laws

Zoning laws must be revised.[117] Wheeler writes, "Rethinking zoning must be a key element of sustainability planning."[118] Sprawl and all the problems of single-use developments will only get worse under current zoning laws in most areas. Zoning laws have nothing to do with livability or helping the poor improve their lives. The poor have been completely eliminated from the picture when it comes to zoning low-income neighborhoods. In fact, almost everybody has been left out of the process. New Urbanism advocate Eric Jacobsen writes, "Zoning laws in existence in most cities today were not forged out of any kind of a public process, but were developed (or copied from a template) by engineers and city bureaucrats who care more about predictable patterns and neat categories than charm and neighborhood ethos."[119]

Part of the problem is that single-use is assumed to be the desired norm. Jane Jacobs writes, "The desirability of segregating dwellings from work has been so dinned into us that it takes an effort to look at real life and observe that residential districts lacking mixture with work do not fare well in cities."[120] We need to take off the blinders that have shaped neighborhood design for far too long and acknowledge the failure of single-use zoning.

The most important change that needs to happen in terms of zoning laws is to allow businesses and homes in the same neighborhood and even in the same building. Even the UN sees the value of mixed-use communities.

Most bylaws and regulations promote the concept of segregated land use. But poor households often set up shops and workplaces within their homes. Much of this activity is in the informal sector, although it may serve formal sector enterprises. In the absence of other options, this is the only means by which most slum dwellers can make a living. These violations make poor communities vulnerable to corruption and police violence. Mixed land use should be legalized in low-income settlements and investment promoted for economically productive activities and the development of skills.[121]

Mixed-use zoning needs to become the standard and single-use the exception not the other way around. This is true for all nations including the US and other advanced economies. If America's low-income neighborhoods were mixed-use, they would be spared the violence and decay that is a chronic problem in cities across the United States.[122]

Even though most zoning laws are racist and classist, some do serve an important purpose. The removal of zoning laws altogether could potentially put the poor and the environment at risk. Governments need to institute policies to ensure that there are enough houses for the entire population. Wheeler writes, "Affordable units have been in woefully short supply in many metropolitan areas in recent decades, since for-profit housing developers prefer to build middle- and upper-income housing rather than low-income units."[123] No one should have to live without a house while large homes sit vacant waiting for someone wealthy enough to purchase it.

The environment could be at great risk if owners could do whatever they want on the land. Los Angeles is facing the consequences of zoning exemptions that have allowed an energy company to operate oil wells within the city. Not surprisingly, the company acts without concern for the community. Residents that have become sick find themselves against a company that denies all responsibility for causing any health problems. Zoning laws need to regulate businesses that are not owner occupants.

Zoning laws should be used to ensure the preservation of forests, wildlife reserves, and agricultural land. This is done by incentivizing urban growth and limiting development in other areas. Agricultural land and forests should not be parceled out and sold for development.

The major land use distinction for zoning should be urban and rural instead of residential and commercial. Urban land needs to be a development priority and rural land a conservation priority. This revision of zoning laws will ensure the density needed for vibrant urban life, as well as the preservation of agricultural land.

The elimination of the residential and commercial dichotomy allows for flexible land use that helps both residents and businesses. It gets rid of the unnecessary red tape and lets people make decisions without jumping through hoops.

Policies that Work to Improve the Lives of Society's Most Vulnerable

Community-Driven Regulation

Environmental Science professor Dara O'Rourke describes a valuable model for environmental regulations in what he calls community-driven regulations (CDR). This model is based on the understanding that residents in communities that suffer directly from environmental degradation engage in the political arena to get results. The community-driven regulations model uses the power of concerned citizens with an immediate felt need to bring about actual change.

> The CDR process leads to more than just pro forma actions. Community members in general are much more interested in results—that is, pollution reduction—than in inspections, reports, EIA's, or even agreements to build treatment plants. Mobilized communities thus serve as an expansive team of monitors to follow up on inspections and promises of improvement. This is particularly important, as monitoring and follow-up are the Achilles' heel of traditional top-down environmental regulations.[124]

Community-driven regulation works in many areas of community life in informal settlements beyond environmental issues. Building codes, land use, businesses, and food safety are all regulated in informal settlements by the residents themselves. Businesses are regulated based on their noise, pollution, and impact on neighbors. An Internet café that temporarily opened on my walkway was forced to move when a neighbor complained about the noise and number of teenagers loitering in the walkway. Neighbors also regulate building safety. Fire safety is so ingrained in the residents that they are always on the lookout for potential dangers. This makes community-driven regulation better than government sponsored fire inspections.

Community-driven regulation already naturally happens within the context of an informal settlement. The community-driven regulation model must be integrated into the policy of local governments. This shifts the role of the government from command and control to training, equipping, and providing the legal structure for concerned citizens to better legislate, regulate, and enforce policies that work to improve their lives.

Don't Force the Poor Into Isolation

The model of warehousing the poor fails to help them improve their lives. It adds hardship to the poor by forcing them into isolation. In Vancouver's Downtown Eastside "82 percent of the neighborhood housing was limited to single room occupancies (SROs)—tiny, cockroach-infested apartments. It was little wonder that so many turned to drugs to dull the pain."[125] Some tiny house communities can also force the poor into isolation if they are limited to single occupancy. Forcing the poor to live alone has its consequences. It is "the state most associated with unhappiness and poor mental health."[126]

The perpetual shortage of affordable houses is a direct cause of some homelessness and overcrowding. When all of the available housing options are too expensive, the only choice people have is to squeeze into an expensive home and split the costs. The poor squeeze into living space because they do not have any other option. Multiple families live together because none of them can afford to move out. When affordable housing units increase, overcrowding will naturally decrease.

Forcing the poor into isolation is directly related to the obsession of preventing overcrowding. Wealthy politicians try to stop overcrowding by putting legal limits on how many people can occupy a dwelling, to the point of designating some units as single occupancy. Single occupancy units force the poor into isolation and criminalize them for seeking a basic human need, companionship.

Anti-overcrowding laws criminalize poverty and reveal total ignorance of the on the ground reality of the constituents that politicians are supposed to represent. Overcrowding is not a criminal issue; it is a failed city policy issue. The problem of overcrowding is best addressed through building communities that are specifically designed to help the poor overcome poverty. There is no other way to ensure an abundant supply of affordable housing.

Don't Prevent Mixed-Income Communities

Communities built for the poor often have income limits for someone to live there. This is the exact opposite of mixed-income. It also punishes people for finding good jobs and getting raises by increasing their rent and eventually making them move.

Communities need to be designed to help the poor overcome poverty; therefore there should not be an income limit to live there. They must be truly mixed-income. An important value in informal settlements is the desire to stay even when their income gives them the chance to move out. This is so vital that renowned urban activist Jane Jacobs writes, "The key link in a perpetual slum is that too many people move out of it too fast-and in the meantime dream of getting out. This is the link that has to be broken if any other efforts at overcoming slums, or slum life are to be of the least avail."[127] The whole community will stagnate and fail if people are forced out after they find good jobs or their businesses are established.

Don't Force the Poor to Live in an Upper Class Neighborhood

Upper class neighborhoods are communities of single-family homes and car ownership. These communities meet the desires of the upper class. They are well suited for those with the resources to enjoy the best of suburban living. The residents benefit from their community because it gives property owners some control over property value. Car ownership is desired because driving greatly expands the choice of where to work, shop, or spend leisure time. The wealthy also do not need to supplement their income with a home-based business so mixed-use is not desired. The problem is that the same things that work in favor of the upper class hurts the poor.

It is no wonder why suburbanites hate the city and especially low-income neighborhoods. This hatred is not the fault of the city. It is because suburbanites experience the city the same way they do the suburbs, from their car. Suburbanites who drive to the city experience their greatest driving nightmares; narrow roads, traffic, and limited parking. Therefore, they write off cities as bad places to live and simply assume that everyone benefits from car dependent communities. The real beauty of city living is the freedom from needing a car.

Just because something is important for the rich and middle class does not automatically mean it benefits everyone. The length of their neighbor's grass and the condition of the exterior of their home are not the top priorities of the poor. The poor do not complain about dandelions in their neighbor's yard. They worry about where their next meal will come from. The property value of the place where they are living is not a high priority. Communities for the poor need to be designed based on the needs of the poor, not the values of the upper classes.

Not forcing the poor into an upper class neighborhood means not designing communities for cars and not requiring lawns. It is important to distinguish between what people like and what they are forced into. In many places, Americans are forced to have a lawn because they are not allowed to build right next to the sidewalk. Jane Jacobs criticized city planners' love affair with grass. She sarcastically writes, "The great object of city planning was that Christopher Robin might go hoppety-hoppety on the grass."[128] Interestingly, most people I know that have grass tend to complain about it, but they cannot imagine life any other way.

The assumption that a house must have a lawn is so ingrained that even the extremely poor are forced to have grass. Many localities are turning to tiny homes as a way to reduce homelessness. This is great if the community is designed based on the needs of the residents. However, the number of tiny home parks that are full of grass shows that decision makers are not designing communities to help the poor overcome poverty.

Lawns are an extra burden for the poor. They are essentially dead space that needs to be maintained but does not help them overcome poverty. The visual pleasantness of looking at green grass does not justify the financial burden it places on the poor.

Beyond dealing with grass, vacant space between buildings is costly. Every square foot of lawn lowers the population density of a community. Lawns expand the distance needed to travel to school, work, or shop. This in turn makes a community less walkable and encourages car use. Front yards hinder the ability to meet neighbors. Sitting on a porch right along the sidewalk allows for natural conversation with anyone who walks by the house. When the home and sidewalk are separated by a front yard, a smile and wave is all that can happen.

The poor have completely different needs and therefore the communities they live in must be designed differently. Instead of every home needing to have a lawn, public multi-use fields should be dispersed throughout neighborhoods. Detached single-family homes do not help the poor improve their lives and therefore should be avoided in communities meant to serve the poor. The design must include the freedom to build their homes and use the buildings in ways that best meets the needs of a family.

Prioritize Pedestrians, Bikes, and Public Transit

The transportation budget greatly favors the upper classes over the poor. "Almost eighty cents of every federal transportation dollar already goes to highway building and road maintenance, which obviously discriminates against people who aren't affluent enough to own cars."[129] Public transit receives pennies on the dollar compared to the welfare subsidy for highways.

The priority of cars is made clear by the amount of public land and money designated for roads. When pedestrians, bikes, and public transit are prioritized, driving will become less appealing. As people lose their desire to drive they need viable alternatives. Walking, biking, and public transit all need to be developed so that people do not have to drive. Speck writes, "Every city has an obligation to free its residents from the burden of auto dependence."[130]

Communities centered on pedestrians, bikes, and public transit help the poor. The UN Millennium Project Task Force on Improving the Lives of Slum Dwellers verified that, "Bylaws and regulations invariably cater to automobiles. Since there are few automobiles in low-income settlements, such roads serve little purpose and adversely affect community social life."[131] Giving citizens the freedom to design their communities in ways that meet their needs allows people—not cars—to be served by their community.

One mayor who was determined to shift his city's policy away from private cars to pedestrians, bikes, and public transit was Enrique Penalosa. The city of Bogota has an annual No Car Day where all private vehicles including motorcycles are banned from the roads. "From 5:00 am until 7:30 pm today, more than two million cars that normally fill Bogota won't be able to circulate on the streets of the Colombian capital during the first official 'No Car Day' of 2017."[132] The event was started by Mayor Penalosa in 2000 and was so popular that it was made into an annual event.

If a community is going to serve its low-income residents, it must be walkable. Roseland writes, "The design and construction of a walkable community provides the most affordable transportation system any community can plan and maintain."[133] Walkable communities save the poor much needed money that can go to other vital areas of their life.

Public transportation provides a great service for the poor and elderly, but its ridership should not be limited to those without other options. There needs to be a wide variety of convenient and affordable options to travel throughout a metro area. The transit system needs to be the best option in terms of affordability, convenience, speed, and an overall enjoyable experience. It needs to be so good that even those who own cars will sometimes choose to take public transit because it is the fastest and most convenient way to travel.

Prioritize High-Density

Urban areas need to prioritize high-density. This is not a popular idea. Jane Jacobs sums up the general anti-density mentality, "This is a common assumption: that human beings are charming in small numbers and noxious in large numbers."[134] High-density is treated as if it is the plague that needs to be avoided at all costs.

Prioritizing high-density is based on the understanding that high concentrations of people are needed for mixed-use and walkable communities. Without high-density, home-based stores are hard to maintain. Rybczynski writes, "The success of a shopping street, a city park, or a waterfront esplanade depends on the presence of large numbers of people."[135] High-density makes all the necessary features of a neighborhood that serve the poor possible.

It is important to note that citywide population densities can be misleading because the statistic can include unused land on the outer rim of the city. In terms of population density it is specific neighborhoods that should strive for high-density, not necessarily an entire area. Healthy population density also balances mixed-use and public space.

Living Where You Serve

Living where you serve is non-negotiable in order for communities to help low-income residents overcome poverty. The wisdom to live where you serve is not new. Lao Tzu, an ancient Chinese philosopher said:

Go to the people.

Live with them.

Learn from them.

Love them.

Start with what they know.

Build with what they have.

But with the best leaders,

when the work is done,

the task accomplished,

the people will say

'We have done this ourselves.'[136]

The wisdom is so basic. Effective leadership begins with living among the people. In modern times, it is possible to live in an entirely different location from the one supposedly being served. Policy makers, city planners, and architects are all relatively wealthy. From the perspective of the poor, they are rich. Policy makers write laws that exploit the poor not because they like to see people suffer, but because they simply assume that their lifestyle is normal. Korten writes, "There is good reason to conclude that people who are isolated from the daily reality of those they rule are ill prepared to define the public interest."[137] The poor have a wide range of needs that are virtually unrecognizable by anyone who is not poor. The only way to truly understand how the poor live is to live among them, love them, and learn from them. After spending years living in the slums of Phnom Penh and Vancouver, social activist Craig Greenfield writes, "Our isolation from the poor shapes how we understand poverty, and it drives how we respond to it."[138] As much as we would like to shortcut the process, there is simply no way to design neighborhoods that meet the needs of the poor without actually experiencing life from their perspective.

When the people who design communities for the poor do not live among the poor, the neighborhood is not going to help the poor overcome of poverty. Those designing low-income communities need to live in a slum with their families if they are truly serious about designing communities that help the poor overcome poverty.

Police, social workers, teachers, school administrators, city planners, county supervisors, and city council members should all be required to live in the low-income neighborhood they are paid to serve. Everyone who is involved in policy making, the whole way up the political hierarchy including the mayor, need to live in a low-income community. In order to move away from being a plutocracy (rule by the rich) and back to a true democracy, politicians need to move out of their elite gated subdivisions and back to reality with the rest of the people.

In order to make this happen, job contracts need to include the stipulation of living where you serve. Some cities already require their employees to live within city limits. This is a start but it needs to be expanded to require some employees to live in low-income communities.

Businesses Friendly

Governments need to shift from favoring large businesses to giving small businesses a fighting chance. This includes legal protection for mixed-use communities that allow the residents to operate businesses from their homes.

Policies need to make starting a business as easy as possible. Business owners in high-density, walkable, mixed-use, mixed-income neighborhoods should be able to open their enterprises from their home without a permit. A minimal annual fee could be collected as long as it is small enough not to discourage potential businesses. Small home-based businesses should not have to deal with sales tax because when they purchase the supplies used for their businesses they pay sales tax on those goods. The only limitations would be strong odors and real safety concerns such as selling products that already require special permits.

Subsidies for Everyone's Benefit

Walkable neighborhoods are cost efficient because they require less government subsidies for roads and parking lots. Those living in high-density, walkable, mixed-income communities should receive the same government funds as they would have received for road building and maintenance. Gallagher writes, "suburban development itself—everything from the federal highway system to the single-family home to the low price of gasoline in the United States compared to other countries—was built thanks to, and still depends on, generous government subsidies."[139]

Subsidizing the poor needs to be much smarter than the current welfare system in which almost everyone loses. The poor are trapped in a system of dependency that punishes them for taking steps to improve their lives and public funds are wasted on maintaining the status quo. It would be cheaper and better for the poor if subsidies moved away from food assistance and oppressive public housing to truly helping the poor improve their lives so that eventually they will not need the subsidy.

Communities that help the poor overcome poverty must receive the standard benefits of every other community such as paved walkways, streetlights, sewage, and drainage systems. The residents should also receive subsidies in the form of grants for land rights and vouchers for construction supplies.

Active Involvement Not Laissez-faire

At times, some of these policies might feel so laissez-faire that someone who is usually anti-government might disapprove, while others could be accused of being too regulation-driven or big government. In reality, neither the far right nor the far left would result in sustainable and livable neighborhoods that help the poor improve their lives. The government needs to be actively involved; yet on the other hand, there is no room for oppressive and burdensome ordinances. Government involvement needs to focus on infrastructure development and working with the residents to create jobs. The local residents can be encouraged to invest locally by providing subsidies and tax breaks for cottage industry and other home-based businesses.

Change is Possible

Some of these policy adjustments might seem impossible. There is no denying that it is an uphill battle to change oppressive laws. The reason why the world is the way it is today is because powerful people like it that way. The fight is against a well-funded establishment with an agenda to maintain the status quo.

There are classist and slumophobic prejudices that need to be overcome. Those who are anti-informal settlements and tent city need a paradigm shift, similar to the one needed by racists and anyone who hates what they do not understand.

The hope that change is possible is based on the fact that only two major changes are needed. Society as a whole needs a paradigm shift in the way we view the purpose of communities. Homes and the neighborhoods in which they are located need to move away from being a financial investment for property owners to being places that improve the lives of the residents. There also needs to be a change in the legal structure.

The most encouraging fact that change is possible is that the world's informal settlers prove that high-density, walkable, mixed-use, mixed-income communities can help people overcome poverty and add to the residents' quality of life. It is time to stop simply doing things just because that is how they have always been done. Montgomery writes, "We can make cities that are more generous and less cruel. We can make cities that help us all get stronger, more resilient, more connected, more active, and more free. We just have to decide who our cities are for. And we have to believe that they can change."[140] Oppressing the poor through community design needs to stop. There is a way to move forward. We just need to start implementing the wisdom of informal settlements.

12

The Slum Without the Symptoms of Poverty

Poverty is dehumanizing. It is grinding and painful. Poverty sucks the life out of people by preventing them from reaching their full potential. Poverty makes people vulnerable to predators who oppress and exploit the weak for their own gain. Some of the oppressive practices are horrifying. In my younger days, I used to ask people why they keep working under such conditions. "My family needs to eat" was the common response. When the choice is working to the bone for almost nothing or the starvation of their children there is really no option, they have to work in exploitative situations.

Poverty is extremely complicated and multifaceted. There is no one-size-fits-all response to poverty. Many different areas need to be addressed in the fight against global poverty. One chapter and not even a single book is enough to discuss all of the ways that people overcome poverty. In this chapter, I will only focus on designing communities that actually help the poor. Local politicians and city planners need to take responsibility for designs that hurt the poor and begin to see their work as a vital element in addressing poverty in their jurisdiction.

Many other vital areas need to be addressed in a holistic plan to help the poor improve their lives. Designing neighborhoods that are high-density, walkable, mixed-use, and mixed-income is only one part of the solution. It is not the silver bullet that will help every household suffering from poverty.

New approaches to neighborhood design can help reduce poverty and give the poor more control of their lives. As Neuwirth writes, "Give squatters security and they will develop the cities of tomorrow."[141] They know their needs and they know how to address them. All they really need is the legal structure to protect them from oppression and sometimes a little help to get started.

Common Mistakes

Governments tend to view slums as problems to be solved. The response to slums is therefore an attempt to fix something that is broken as opposed to strengthening what works. Fixing slums is done in one of two ways. The first is to demolish the slum and relocate the residents to a built for the poor community or provide rent vouchers for them to live in a middle-class community. The second is to do some type of on-site slum upgrade project. Both of these are mainly about hiding poverty so the upper classes do not have to see the poor. These responses do not help the poor improve their lives.

Demolition

Demolition is when the homes and businesses of the poor are intentionally destroyed. When the poor build tent cities and informal settlements to solve the housing shortage, instead of being thanked and rewarded by the government their homes are destroyed.

America has a zero tolerance policy for any effort by the poor to build their own housing. Tent cities are usually brutally destroyed before they have a chance to establish themselves.

Problems of poverty are confused with the slums themselves. The easy solution is to destroy the places where poor people live. In the US, "tearing down slum housing was seen as a way of destroying the crime, delinquency, drunkenness, and lax morals that were considered to be associated with the slum housing."[142]

Under the guise of "urban renewal" US cities demolished slums and dislocated thousands of the city's poorest and most vulnerable residents who were moved to public housing projects. These were supposed to solve all of the problems associated with slums, but they turned out to be worse than the original neighborhoods that were destroyed. Jane Jacobs writes, "A Pittsburgh study, undertaken to show the supposed clear correlation between better housing and improved social conditions, compared delinquency records in still uncleared slums to delinquency records in new housing projects, and came to the embarrassing discovery that the delinquency was higher in the improved housing."[143] The lesson to be learned is that just because a neighborhood looks nicer from the outside does not mean that the lives of the poor have improved. Sadly, politicians still seem to think that destroying poor people's homes is the way to go. The current solution to the problems of housing projects is to destroy the buildings that housed the poor and try again.

Demolition is not a real solution. Jane Jacobs writes, "At best, it merely shifts slums from here to there, adding its own tincture of extra hardship and disruption. At worst, it destroys neighbourhoods where constructive and improving communities exist and where the situation calls for encouragement rather than destruction."[144]

Built for the poor communities, even ones that are absolute disasters in terms of design should not be demolished. The disruption caused by demolition usually outweighs any benefit to the redesign of a community. Demolition does not help the poor improve their lives and overcome poverty.

Demolition is such violence against the poor that those ordering such actions are self-deceived by lies used to confuse reality. Demolition adds to the suffering of the poor, yet it is often framed in a way that it is for their good. Those ordering the demolitions appear to actually believe that they are somehow doing what is best for the poor. This is self-deception, believing something that is not true in order to justify harmful actions against another human being.[145] The most common lies used to justify demolition are the safety of the residents, environmental protection, and humanitarian concerns.

The Safety of the Residents

The safety of the residents is a popular excuse for destroying communities built by the poor. It makes the government appear to be concerned about the welfare of the residents. In reality, most of the time the area is not as unsafe as it is portrayed to be. The only time this excuse is valid is a situation of a hidden danger like the Chernobyl nuclear disaster that released deadly radiation into the surrounding area.

I lived in the railroad community of Balic-Balic, Manila for seven years until it was demolished for the safety of the residents and to upgrade the train system. The first reaction by those who did not live in the community was that the area must be dangerous because the homes were built within a few feet from active train tracks. Ironically, no one from the community shared this concern. The train was treated with respect. Whenever the whistle was heard in the distance, people would shout "train!" until everyone cleared the tracks. Right after the train passed everyone stepped back on the tracks and life continued as usual.

In the seven years that I lived along the tracks, I only know of one person who was killed by the train in my community. Others were killed in different locations along the tracks, some of which were suicides by people outside the neighborhood. One accidental death in seven years hardly makes a community dangerous. If every neighborhood were judged by the same standards, no community would be deemed safe.

Forbidding building with cement is a common practice among landowners to limit informal settlers. The result is a community built entirely of flammable materials. City officials are quick to recognize the fire hazard and recommend demolition. Instead of changing unjust laws that prevent the use of safer building materials the community is simply destroyed. The demolition is justified because of conditions artificially created by laws that prevent the poor from improving their community.

Environmental Protection

Environmental protection is another common excuse for destroying the communities of the poor. Demolishing the homes of the poor in order to protect the environment is usually related to programs designed to clean waterways. The poor that build their homes along waterways are blamed for trash thrown in the water. The poor do throw their trash in the water, but they are certainly not the only ones. There are also much less destructive solutions such as improved trash service and education. Those concerned about environmental issues need to work with the residents for a win-win solution. With outside help and resources, most residents would be more than happy to comply with environmental legislation that in turn improves their community.

The self-deception of using environmental protection to justify demolition is based on the myth that informal settlements are harmful for the environment. As was already examined, high-density communities do less overall damage to the environment, but the damage they do cause is noticed in the immediate area. Relocating residents might help clean up that specific area, however if they are moved to a typical built for the poor community, not only will the residents be worse off, but they will also do more overall environmental damage.

Humanitarian Concerns

When there is no logical way to challenge the residents' safety or claim environmental protection the last resort is rooted in humanitarian concerns. This is usually framed something like, "subhuman housing" or "no human being should live in those conditions." Destitute living conditions do exist and we need to do everything possible to address poverty. However, more often than not, those same "subhuman" living conditions are the result of oppression.

I have a neighbor who was forced to stop building a third floor out of non-flammable cement. Now the third floor sits unfinished. The building materials exposed to the elements causes them to rapidly deteriorate and serves as the perfect excuse to destroy the whole community.

Homes in informal settlements and tent cities should not be categorized as subhuman housing. A home, no matter how small or pathetic it might look is still better than sleeping outside without any shelter. There are individual homes that need improvements to make them more comfortable, but simply having a small, or "ugly" house does not make it a place unfit for habitation. It is complete arrogance to claim that an entire community is subhuman. The isolation caused by elite gated communities can also be described as subhuman housing, because they prevent healthy social interaction needed for our well-being. Of course, no one is trying to demolish homes that earn the government money in the form of real estate taxes.

The Jungle, a built by the poor community in San Jose, CA was a place where the formerly homeless could take steps to improve their lives. "Most of the people who live there didn't choose to be homeless, but now that they are, the Jungle meets their most basic needs."[146] The community was humble, but it met the needs of the residents. To the shame of San Jose, the power holders were blinded by slumophobia and destroyed the community.

The Jungle was demolished on December 4, 2014 under the guise of all three excuses. The San Jose homelessness response manager, "cited the rain as well as other factors such as increased violence and unsanitary conditions as the immediate pretext for the eviction. Within the past month, one resident attempted to strangle another with a cord of wire, while another was nearly beaten to death with a hammer."[147] In most neighborhoods when there are assaults, the police arrest the perpetrators. In the case of the

Jungle, the city destroyed the whole neighborhood. The double standard is obvious becomes no city government would demolish a wealthy community because of domestic violence. The concern of rain is another weak excuse. There are many cheaper and less destructive ways to keep the residents safe in the event of flooding such as dredging the creek so that it can hold more water or to build embankments so the residents can build their homes higher up.

The Jungle's demolition was also tied to environmental protection. "Trying to present the displacement as a process of environmental renewal, the State Water Resources Control Board celebrates the fact that nearby Coyote Creek will finally be cleaned of debris and human excrement."[148] The State Water Resources Control Board celebrating environmental renewal is understandable. I can relate to their joy, but the costs were massive for the residents of the Jungle. They lost their homes and possessions. I am sure none of the members of the State Water Resources Control Board would celebrate the destruction of their own home, regardless of how good it would be for the environment. I visited the Jungle a year after its destruction and Coyote Creek is definitely still polluted. Destroying the homes of the poor did not magically clean the water.

There are many less destructive alternatives. The residents could have been given grants to install toilets in their homes and/or constructing public toilets could have solved the problem of human excrement in the creek. A better trash collection system by the government could have kept the area free from debris. The environmental destruction caused by the Jungle was the fault of the San Jose city government for depriving the community of basic services.

San Jose's homelessness response manager also said, "This site is no longer open for any individuals. The fact that anyone has to live in conditions like this is horrible. This shouldn't be a viable alternative for anyone. We need to make sure that people never have to live in a place like this."[149] This comment reflects a misunderstanding of the potentials of informal settlements and the harsh realities of homelessness. Sleeping in the street without any protection is the real horrible living condition. The residents of the Jungle built their homes and community to meet their needs and to improve their lives. They built a community with great potential had the city supported them instead of persecuting them.

The demolition of the Jungle added to the suffering of the city's most vulnerable residents. The residents were forced out and their belongings confiscated. This was more than an eviction. It was a violent attack by the government on citizens for taking steps to improve their lives. "Eva Martinez, 63, told the *San Jose Mercury News*, 'This is my home. Now I'll have to lay down on the street, somewhere outside. I couldn't bring out all of my stuff. The rest will end up in the dumpsters, I guess. It's terrible. It's terrible for all of us.'"[150] Martinez sums up demolition with precision and clarity. It's terrible for all of us.

On-Site Slum Improvement

The other common approach to deal with the "problem" of slums is on-site improvement. Slum upgrade projects tend to have the goal of turning a slum into a middle-class neighborhood. I visited a community that was in the process of an on-site "upgrading" project. The original informal settlement was built for pedestrians, but the new neighborhood was built for cars even though the residents did not own cars. Roads take up much more space than walkways, so the upgrade project meant that many people were forced to move. While standing on the freshly paved street I asked one of the remaining residents what happened to the family who used to live in the exact spot where we were standing. She replied, "They had to sacrifice for development." The on-site slum improvement project was causing divisions among former neighbors and intensified the hardships for the residents. Both those who were evicted and those who were the so-called beneficiaries no longer lived in a community designed to help them overcome poverty.

The UN-Habitat has a very strange description of slum upgrading.

Upgrading consists of regularization of the rights to land and housing and improving the existing infrastructure—for example, water supply (& storage), sanitation, storm drainage and electricity—up to a satisfactory standard. Typical upgrading projects provide footpaths and pit latrines, street lighting, drainage and roads, and often water supply and limited sewerage. Usually, upgrading does not involve home construction, since the residents can do this themselves.[151]

I call this a strange description because they define upgrading as providing basic services that every upper class community automatically gets. Upper class communities with publicly funded streetlights are not described as the beneficiaries of an upgrading project. True upgrading involves going beyond providing minimal infrastructure and services.

The focus of upgrading is often on aesthetics as if an ugly home is the definition of poverty. It is as if all the poor need are attractive homes and they will live happily ever after. This is one reason why slum upgrade projects fail. As the saying goes, "never judge a book by its cover." We must never look at a dirty cluster of shanties that the poor built themselves and assume the community is a bad place to live. In all likelihood, it is helping the residents better cope with the difficulties of poverty. In the same way we must never judge a slum upgrade project by how much nicer the homes look.

I have listened to the coordinators of slum upgrade projects boastfully show before and after pictures of what the informal settlement looked like when the residents built it themselves, and the freshly constructed housing. Yes, the new homes are painted and nicely aligned along organized streets, but does the newly built neighborhood meet the holistic needs of the residents like the original community did? Does it enhance relationships, and encourage business startups? Sadly, the original communities that were destroyed were better for the poor than the new ones built for them.

Solutions to Poverty Not Slums

There are issues within informal settlements that should be addressed and certainly not replicated. At the same time it is important to emphasize that it is poverty that needs eliminated, not the positive features of informal settlements. The focus of informal settlements needs to shift. Far from being problems to be solved, informal settlements are assets to be strengthened.

Integrating the Informal Economy

The informal economy defined as businesses that operate under the radar of the government needs to be decriminalized and integrated into mainstream society. There is a lot of misunderstanding and outright hostility when it comes to the informal economy. Gottdiener and Budd write, "The informal economy may involve activities that are not only illegal because they use undocumented workers or are off the books, they may also involve criminal acts in their own right. Illegal activities in the informal economy include drug trafficking, people smuggling, money laundering, gambling and prostitution."[152] Their negative view of the informal economy leads to harsh laws that devastate the poor. This definition is geared toward organized crime with millionaire crime bosses not someone selling school supplies from their home.

The informal economy in informal settlements is someone trying to earn a supplemental income in order to feed their children. While there is certainly illegal economic activity in informal settlements, the vast majority are businesses that contribute to the welfare of the community. Journalist Mark Kramer writes, "Informal settlements represent a system of survival created by people who cannot afford the time and expense of working through massive bureaucracies or obeying the law when designing a home or business because the law is antiquated and ignores on-the-ground realities of poor people."[153]

Integrating the informal economy is how governments can work for the people. Economist

Hernando de Soto writes of the situation in Peru:

> We face two challenges: what can we do to prevent informal
> energies from being kept in check by a punitive legal system
> and how can we transfer the vitality, persistence, and hopes of
> the emerging business class to the rest of the country? The
> answer is to change our legal institutions in order to lower the
> cost of producing and obtaining wealth, and to give people
> access to the system so they can join in economic and social
> activity and compete on an equal footing, the ultimate goal
> being a modern market economy which, so far, is the only
> known way to achieve development based on widespread
> business activity.[154]

De Soto's questions are not just for Peru. They need to be answered anywhere zoning laws and other legislation punishes the poor for trying to improve their lives.

The informal economy is not a side effect of underdevelopment. It is alive and well in the US and other developed nations. Even though it is viciously opposed, some are still able to run underground businesses in the US. The poor in the US do engage in business. Poverty in the US would be reduced if the government encouraged the economic activity of the poor instead of criminalizing it.

Informality provides the poor the freedom they need to engage in a wide variety of business options. It is within the environment of community-driven regulations that the poor have been able to develop communities that meet their needs and help them to improve their lives.

South African Research Chair in Urban Policy Edgar Pieterse writes,

> Any slum improvement intervention must be sober about why
> it may be beneficial for some people to want to continue their
> livelihoods in a context of an informal settlement and not
> formal housing or a more formalized environment. As slums

exist currently, they are teeming with life, social networks and economic linkages. It is often impossible to re-create these livelihood options and possibilities outside the highly fluid and malleable physical conditions that are best offered by informal areas.[155]

Integrating the informal economy can be done by eliminating single-use zoning and by giving small-scale home-based businesses the freedom to start without government paperwork. The recognition and decriminalization of the informal economy protects the poor from corrupt police and other government official seeking bribes. It would also allow non-profits and banks to provide micro-loans for home-based businesses.

Land Ownership

Owning and occupying land are fuzzy concepts. Does ownership depend on a piece of paper with stamps and signatures, or actually living on the land? The middle class view land ownership as purchasing a piece of land validated by a title authorized by the government. The land ownership values of the middle class are not universal.

In many ways, informal settlers do not actually need land ownership. Neuwirth writes, "Security, stability, protection, and control are what's important."[156] As long as they have some assurance that their home will not be demolished, life continues as normal. Home repairs are made as money becomes available and the community slowly improves. Neuwirth also writes, "Squatters build and rebuild and build again without a title deed. They don't need one to secure their future. They simply need a sense of control over their homes and a guarantee that they will not be arbitrarily evicted."[157]

When informal settlers are granted land titles, they have extra expenses in the form of mortgages and property taxes. In reality, they do not actually get anything new because they were already using the land. Land ownership can also force the poor to enter the world of building codes, zoning laws, and government red tape, which under the current system will add to their hardship.

On the other hand, land ownership is how the poor can be assured that they will not be forced out of their homes. In order to help informal settlers own their land without burdening them with expensive mortgages, public funds should be made available to subsidize all or most of the purchase price. Land grants could be given to informal settlers and tent city residents. UN Millennium Project Task Force on Improving the Lives of Slum Dwellers conclude that, "The poor rarely have the resources to purchase land; making land available at nominal or no cost is the beginning of most efforts at improving their conditions."[158] Once they are given the assurance that they will not be forced to move, they will invest in their homes and improve their neighborhood.

Land subsidies for informal settlers in high-density, walkable communities balances itself by the fact that the government spends less for public services in these neighborhoods compared to less dense areas. If the government spends money for building and maintaining roads in wealthy neighborhoods, they could help the poor purchase the small piece of land where their home is located.

Homeownership

Homeownership is different for the poor than it is for the middle and upper classes. Homeownership is an investment for the middle class and thus they have a high priority for property value. Homes are bought with high hopes that property values will increase and they will earn a profit on its eventual sale. The poor, on the other hand, do not build homes in tent cities or informal settlements as investments they hope to make money on. They build homes so their families can have a safe place to sleep every night. It also gives them stability and frees them from the burden of paying rent.

Homeownership can be a stepping-stone out of poverty. A neighborhood designed for low-income families to become homeowners is one that helps the poor improve their lives. Based on his experience in the US, community developer John Perkins writes:

> An important way to help people turn themselves into valuable assets is to make home ownership possible. Many businesses start when people take out loans against the value of their homes. Most of the wealth of middle- and working-class people is invested in their houses. A house can also be sold after a period of appreciation to generate more wealth. When children inherit houses the opportunity for economic strength in the second generation is greatly increased.[159]

A family can own a home and still suffer from poverty. They could also over buy and become burdened by debt. In other cases, a home can be purchased at or even below what a family would normally pay for rent. When a family owns their home, they do not have to worry about being evicted or finding affordable rent. Slumlords would not be able to exploit the poor's inability to purchase a home.

Owning a home automatically means that you have a vested interest in the welfare of the community. As a renter, there is not much motivation to get involved in community projects, because if the community improves too much, it will gentrify and you will no longer be able to afford to live there. Community improvements work in the favor of homeowners.

Once a person becomes a homeowner, their view of their house begins to shift. All of a sudden home improvement projects begin to gain importance. As a renter, you just live with what you get. As a homeowner, you will spend money on improving your home. This includes the unwanted expense of general upkeep, but there are also other improvements that make the home more comfortable. Home improvements in informal settlements are done based on practicality without concern for how it will impact the value of the home.

The decision to rent or buy should be left up to the families themselves and not dictated by politicians who determine to have rental only communities. Too often, the poor cannot afford homeownership because every house that would be within their price range is not for sale. Government housing projects are constructed and maintained assuming the poor residents will be eternal renters. These units must be available for purchase within the price range of the poor.

If the government is willing to subsidize rent, it must also be willing to help with building materials and mortgages. Rent vouchers need to shift to mortgage vouchers so that homeownership is possible for low-income families. Another way for the poor to become homeowners is by allowing them to construct their own house in their own way.

Access to Education and Employment Opportunities

Education is vital for the long-term future of a community. If the schools are not very good, a community will not be mixed-income because everyone with children and the option to leave the area will move out. Others who might have considered moving into the community will look elsewhere if their children's education is jeopardized.

Educational opportunities should not be limited to children and teenagers. Technical skills training and advanced degrees are all important for helping families out of poverty. Students of all ages need to have access to empowering education.

Employment that pays a livable wage is one of the best and lasting solutions to poverty. On the other hand, exploitative employment that pays virtually slave wages and denies employees the opportunity for advancement perpetuates poverty. Communities must have access to a variety of employment opportunities. They must also be mixed-use so residents have the option to create their own source of income through cottage industry or a home-based business.

When the government is hiring for local positions, the first opportunities should go to local residents. The government should also hire as many people as possible. I visited a large US city and learned that almost everyone on the block where I stayed was unemployed and received some form of government assistance. At the same time, the streets were littered with trash. At least some of those needing work could be hired as street sweepers to both provide employment and to clean up the trash in the community.

Access to Health Care

Access to health care is vital for society. Sickness and disease can greatly diminish quality of life. Health care is not just the concern of an individual sick person. It is a public concern, because if that sick person has an infectious disease, all of society is also at risk. When the poor do not have access to health care, everyone suffers. An outbreak of the flu, drug-resistant TB, or a super-bug is just waiting to happen.

Access to health care includes both the physical distance to doctors' offices and hospitals as well as the ability to pay for medical services. Neighborhood design can ensure that doctors' offices are accessible by walking or a short commute through not having codes and permits that force doctors to work in large centralized hospitals.

Access to health care also includes addressing the neighborhood issues that contribute to an unhealthy environment. Sicknesses in low-income communities are often preventable and caused by governmental neglect. According to the United Nations:

> Ill health in poor communities is normally associated with poor sanitation, lack of waste disposal facilities, the presence of vermin, and poor indoor air quality due to poor ventilation and the use of cheap fuels that emit particulate matter. Accidents, particularly involving children, are also far more common in households with open fires or accessible boiling water, and the

results of these can be horrific when no medical care is available.[160]

Sanitation, waste disposal, air quality, and access to medical care are the responsibility of the government. Sanitation is one of the basic issues of informal settlements. Every household should be helped to have running water and a functioning bathroom. General sanitation measures within a community such as regular trash pickup and enforcing pollution regulations can be established. The health care system needs to be affordable for the residents so that when they do get sick they will seek treatment.

An Inexpensive and Reliable Public Transportation System

Access to public transportation expands the availability of education, employment, and health care. An expensive and limited public transportation system reduces the distance that someone can realistically commute to school or work. On the other hand, a cheap and efficient public transportation system such as bus rapid transit and light rail can greatly expand the distance the poor can commute.

The light rail system that connects Botocan to the rest of the city has greatly enlarged the feasible commuting distance for local residents. A good and inexpensive university is located at the other end of the train line. Before the light rail was built, students from Botocan could not study there because of the cost and time spent commuting. Now there are a number of students in the area who travel back and forth every day via light rail. The light rail system has also connected residents to high paying jobs in the business district.

Protection from Predators

The vulnerability of the poor cannot be overstated. The horror stories of abuse are plentiful. A woman in my old community was forced into sexual slavery by a police officer. She was young and attractive, and like many living in poverty as an adult she still lived with her family. Her father and brothers earned a living by hustling stolen electronics. The officer who

169

tracked her family down was immediately attracted to her and gave her a chance to save her father and brothers from spending the rest of their lives in jail if she would be his on-call sex partner. If she refused, the officer informed her that she would also be arrested. She agreed to the officer's demands and was forced to have sex with him whenever he called.

To be poor is to be vulnerable. The poor do not have the power to stop predators from exploiting them. Slumlords, greedy business owners, politicians, and criminals all take advantage of the vulnerability of the poor. The slums are a source of cheap labor and votes for the unscrupulous. Slumlords buy up property in low-income communities as investments. The initial investment is relatively low and there are almost no upkeep costs so the return on investment is high.

Those who make a living through criminal activity find a safe haven in slums. Gangs hurt small home-based businesses by charging "taxes." This activity is a vicious form of extortion where gangsters use physical threats to ensure payments. The government must protect residents from corrupt police, slumlords, greedy business owners, gangs, and criminals.

Fire Safety

Fire safety is another concern in high-density communities. Fire safety includes the use of nonflammable building materials such as concrete blocks. Residents should be incentivized to build with nonflammable materials. In some cases, these might need to be provided at discounted prices. Infrastructure projects could include the installation of firewalls strategically located throughout the community to ensure that fires are contained.

The local government needs to install and maintain a sufficient number of fire hydrants in the neighborhood. A volunteer fire brigade could be organized and trained so that they could begin putting the fire out well before the fire department arrives. It is already standard practice to install fire hydrants in neighborhoods. The problem is that the residents do not have the equipment or training to take advantage of them. When a fire starts instead of putting it out right away, they have to waste precious minutes waiting for the fire department to arrive.

Development Assistance

The government should provide advisors and funding for infrastructure projects such as sewage, drainage canals, streetlights, CCTV cameras, and paved walkways. Grants and loans should be provided for building materials and small business startups so that a neighborhood can build its economic base.

Microfinance is a popular means of helping the poor start and expand microenterprises around the world. Microfinance and microenterprise development are doing great work at helping households get access to capital. I stayed with a widow in Tegucigalpa, Honduras who was involved in a microfinance program. She used her loan to build four rooms behind her house. I stayed in one of those rooms. The rent she collected went to pay back the loan and the rest was what she lived on for the month. The loan enabled her to have a steady monthly income.

Not everyone benefits from microfinance. Sometimes the loans can burden a household with debt. In some cases, grants are more helpful than loans. A grant would provide the upfront cash to help a business startup.

Grants for education and land rights would also help the poor. Scholarships help relieve some of the financial burden of an education, and enable more students to attend college. Scholarships also help students graduate without huge debt burdens. Grants for land rights help informal settlers become legal landowners and gives them security. Grants can also be used as down payments to help renters in public housing to begin the process of owning their home.

Public and Private Involvement

The government cannot and should not be expected to do everything. The government's role in addressing poverty is to remove oppressive laws and provide legal protection for the poor. The government also has the responsibility of providing funding for education, police protection, infrastructure development, and other basic services. Most people do not want a government handout. They want to be able to earn a living and provide for their families without being harassed and threatened.

Privately funded non-government organizations have an important role to play. Many of these organizations have specific areas of expertise where they are able to make a difference. Some of these organizations provide micro-loans and small business training. Others are involved in helping families construct their home.

Social entrepreneurs and concerned citizens can get involved in a variety of ways by coming alongside the poor in their effort to improve their lives. Architects and engineers can use their skill and expertise to develop durable but inexpensive building materials for the poor to construct their homes.

The public can greatly help the poor by simply changing their class prejudices and stop supporting oppressive policies that cause the poor to suffer. Overcoming prejudices means not being afraid of poor people and intentionally building cross-class friendships. Communities with the specific goal of helping low-income residents overcome poverty need to be advocated for even if it means they are located right next to your neighborhood. Every plan presented by city council members at public meetings needs to be questioned regarding its impact on the poor and minorities. The public must reject the demolition of tent cities and informal settlements and pressure local politicians to work with these communities by providing services and legal protection. Local politicians need to be reminded that the poor are also citizens deserving the full rights of citizenship. In some cases this might mean assisting in voter registration.

13

Sustainable and Livable Neighborhoods for All

I will conclude this book by giving a framework for applying the wisdom of the world's informal settlers in designing sustainable and livable neighborhoods that help the poor overcome poverty. Current built for the poor communities do not serve their needs, but that does not have to be the case. Designers of built for the poor communities can learn from the wisdom of informal settlers in order to design communities that help the poor improve their lives.

The positive aspects of informal settlements should be adopted into the design of neighborhoods. They should be incorporated into a wider area's master plan by designating land throughout a city as walkable, mixed-use, and mixed-income. This would help provide paths out of poverty and better protect the environment.

Walkable, mixed-use, mixed-income communities are most at home in urban areas. The larger urban area surrounding a walkable, mixed-use, mixed-income neighborhood can provide the amenities essential for overcoming poverty. These neighborhoods also have a place in traditional suburban areas. Most suburbs have unused land, so there are areas available that can be developed based on this model. Just like in urban areas, walkable, mixed-use, mixed-income neighborhoods need to be centrally located and near public transportation.

Working with Existing Neighborhoods

The ideal way to fully tap into the strengths of informal settlements is to work with existing ones. Tent cities and informal settlements should be invested in and developed as the assets they are.[161] Built by the poor communities should be partnered with to provide as much assistance as needed and desired.

When informal settlements and tent cities are invested in and the residents are aided in the development of their neighborhood, the area will naturally have enough affordable housing. There will be positive momentum as people have hope that their lives will improve.

Working with tent cities and informal settlements starts with the assets of the residents and builds off the strengths of the community. Services such as water, electricity, sewage, and trash collection need to be provided. Infrastructure projects should also be provided at the request of the residents.

Working with existing neighborhoods that the poor did not build is a different process. It will need to be gradual since there is sure to be pushback along the way. As with any community development initiative, it is important to go at the pace of the community. Once enough influential community leaders catch the vision for transforming their community to one that serves their needs, steps can be taken to start the process.

Most of the work will go into rewriting zoning laws and building codes. Once this major hurdle is overcome, the way has been paved to transition into a walkable, mixed-use, mixed-income community. The prerequisites to these features include high-density, connection to public transportation, and participatory decision-making.

Working with government housing projects requires restructuring so that the management is decentralized. The current board of non-residents needs to be replaced by a governing body of elected community leaders. These leaders must live in the housing project and work directly with city hall. If you do not live in public housing, you have no business serving on a board that dictates how the residents should live.[162]

Residents must also be given the option to purchase their apartment. The units should be priced below market value with generous mortgage options to incentivize homeownership. In order to prevent speculators from buying out the original residents, limits must be placed on how many units can be owned by non-residents. Restrictions may need to be placed on the resale of units.

Neighborhoods need antitrust regulation to provide legal protection from slumlords so the entire community is not controlled by a monopoly of rental units. The percentage paid for property taxes can also increase in proportion to the number of units someone owns. Units owned by non-residents could also be taxed at a higher rate than those owned by residents. This will discourage slumlords from taking over a community.

Even the most pathetically designed public housing communities can be retrofitted to ensure that the neighborhood helps the poor improve their lives. Once residents have more say in their community and are able to purchase their homes they will become more invested in the welfare of their community.

Working with trailer parks and some townhouse and apartment communities involves seeking to help them transition to become high-density, walkable, mixed-use, and mixed-income. Trailer parks can be made high-density by providing incentives to build accessory dwelling units on vacant space between buildings. Multi-story trailers can also be designed to create vertical density. Mixed-income can be achieved by allowing tiny homes as well as houses larger than normal trailers. Trailer parks must give the residents the option to purchase the land where their trailer is located.

These lots also need to be divided in various sizes, giving residents a variety of options.

Most trailer parks are walkable and can easily be made mixed-use through legalizing the opening of businesses from their homes. Depending on the location, the customers do not always have to come from within the community. While visiting the US, I watched a little league baseball game at a neighborhood park. The baseball field was located right next to a trailer park separated by a fence. I could just imagine if that were a typical informal settlement, every home along the fence would have some kind of business. What struck me about this trailer park was the squandering of a great business opportunity simply because the residents were not allowed to operate a business from their homes. If the residents of this community were allowed to run a business from their home, they would be able to increase their monthly income while providing a service to those who use the park.

Working with townhouse or apartment communities may simply require giving the residents the option to purchase units and the freedom to start a home-based business. In many ways, these communities will look about the same as a typical townhouse or apartment community aside from the existence of local businesses and the lack of large parking lots. Parking lots could be turned into more housing or public space such as a park, library, or basketball court.[163] Connecting roads and walkways may also be needed to make the community more accessible.

Designing and Developing New Neighborhoods that Help the Poor Overcome Poverty

The only way to design a neighborhood that helps the poor overcome poverty is for that to be the explicit goal of the community. The lives of the poor will not improve as the side effect of communities designed for other purposes. This must be the starting point for the design of low-income communities.

Thankfully, it is possible to design a community that helps the poor improve their lives. The temptation is to only go halfway. This usually means skipping one of the key components of walkable, mixed-use, mixed-income, healthy population density, and integrated into the broader area. Another way to ensure failure would be to simply fake the key components by having them on paper, but not in actual practice. For this to work to its full potential, communities must go all the way.

When the legal challenge is overcome and the policy revisions discussed in chapter 11 have been adopted for a specific community, new neighborhoods can be designed to help the poor overcome poverty. The neighborhoods should be built for pedestrians. These areas must be designed so that none of the residents need to own cars. These neighborhoods are built with walkways and limited roads. If residents want to own a car, it is their responsibility to find and pay for parking.

These communities should range in size in relation to the city in which they are located. The community needs to be large enough to be truly mixed-use and support a variety of home-based businesses. At the same time, it cannot be too large that it limits a healthy relationship with the rest of the city.

Location is another important aspect of a community's ability to help the poor improve their lives. UN Millennium Project Task Force on Improving the Lives of Slum Dwellers correctly observed that, "The availability of suitable and affordable land in well served, centrally accessible locations is vital for improving the lives of slum dwellers."[164] It is pointless to hide them far from the city. They have to be integrated into the overall plan of the city.

Walkable, mixed-use, mixed-income neighborhoods should be scattered throughout the city starting with the location of current informal settlements and tent cities. Having communities that serve the poor scattered throughout a metro area can ensure enough affordable housing is located near a variety of universities and employers. This will give the poor, students, seniors, and anyone else attracted to the benefits of living in one of these communities a broad range of neighborhoods in the exact location they want to live.

The design of the community should be mainly limited to the layout of the walkways and public space. The walkways should be wide enough to ensure that a wheelchair can easily pass, as well as provide enough space for a safe evacuation in the event of an emergency. Every walkway needs to be accessible by at least two ways. There should not be any dead ends. Walkways also do not have to be a perfect grid since the lots are purchased based on the size desired by the household.

The community should be subdivided with a variety of lot shapes and sizes without a minimum lot or building size. On the contrary, a maximum lot size needs to be established. The issue is not what the building is used for but its size for the community. A building that takes up 5 acres of a 20-acre community does not allow enough diversity for a neighborhood to function properly. Jane Jacobs observed, "On certain streets, any disproportionately large occupant of street frontage is visually a street disintegrator and desolator, although exactly the same *kinds* of uses, at small scale, do no harm and are indeed an asset."[165] In order to overcome this issue, building codes need to put a size limit relative to the size of the community.

The flexibility of lot size needs to be continual. Families need the option of selling a portion of their home when they get desperate so they can address a great need without becoming homeless. How much of the original home the family keeps and how much of it they sell needs to be entirely up to that specific family.

The number of lots that one person can purchase will need to be established to prevent a monopoly and to ensure that the poor do not get outbid by wealthy outsiders and those planning on making money off of the design. The wealthy must be allowed to live there, but it cannot be entirely of people with high incomes or the neighborhood will just become another New Urbanism community that the poor cannot afford.

At this stage safety features such as firewalls and fire hydrants can be installed. Each lot will need to be provided with water and sewage to ensure that every building has running water and a bathroom. Underground drainage canals will also need to be installed in order to prevent flooding.

While households have the freedom to build as they see fit, they should also be aided in designing their homes to best meet their needs. They also need to be given the freedom to build with secondhand material. The government can provide vouchers for construction supplies and NGO's that specialize in helping the poor build their homes can be invited to initiate projects.

Consultants and advisors need to be available to help new or potential residents to fully maximize the features of the community. The consultants need to have actually lived in an informal settlement so they can teach with authority. Advisors can also help families with construction, home design, and business planning.

This brief summary is not meant to be all-inclusive. There are many other areas that specific communities will have to address as they seek to design and develop communities to better serve the residents.

Conclusion

Low-income neighborhoods need to be designed with the explicit goal of helping the residents overcome poverty. Walkable, mixed-use, and mixed-income communities are the best option for neighborhoods that serve the poor. They have the potential to become the standard neighborhood model. These neighborhoods allow the whole area to benefit from the higher population density contributing to a vibrant urban experience for all.

A community is a place that provides housing, but as we saw from the design of informal settlements; it can provide much more than that. A community can also provide employment and social relationships. Slums reimagined can provide livable and sustainable communities for everyone.

This book is designed to get the conversation started. It is not the end of the discussion. County supervisors, city council members, urban planners, architects, community organizers, social workers, religious leaders, small business owners, teachers, schools administrators, and concerned citizens need to be the ones to continue the discussion of designing sustainable and livable neighborhoods that help the poor overcome poverty. Reimagining slums can help us to rethink what communities should offer their residents and how communities can be designed to help the poor improve their lives.

Notes

1 Neuwirth, Robert. *Shadow Cities: A Billion Squatters, a New Urban World*, (New York, NY: Routledge, 2006), 249.

2 Benesh, Sean. *Blueprints for a Just City: The Role of the Church in Urban Planning and Shaping the City's Built Environment*, (Portland, OR: Urban Loft Publishers, 2015), 94-95.

3 Charles, Prince. *A speech by HRH The Prince of Wales at The Prince's Foundation for the Built Environment conference 2009 titled Globalization from the Bottom Up*, (The Prince of Wales and The Duchess of Cornwall, February 5, 2009), Accessed June 15, 2018, https://www.princeofwales.gov.uk/speech/speech-hrh-prince-wales-princes-foundation-built-environment-conference-2009-titled, para. 13.

4 For middle and upper class white people, an unsafe neighborhood is poor and black. This app is both classist and racist.

5 Smith, T. Aaron. *Thriving in the City: A Guide for Sustainable Incarnational Ministry Among the Urban Poor*, (Pomona, CA: Servant Partners Press, 2015), 59-60.

6 United Nations Human Settlements Programme, *The Challenge of Slums: Global Report on Human Settlements 2003*, (London and Sterling, Earthscan Publications Ltd; 2003), 9.

7 Moreno, Eduardo Lopez. and Oyebenji Oyejinka, and Gora Mboup. *State of the World's Cities 2010/2011: Bridging the Urban Divide*, (Sterling VA: Earthscan, 2008), 33.

8 Obviously this is not enough time to accurately assess a community. Yet, most people who make judgments about slums have never actually visited one.

9 In chapter 12, I will discuss the issue of addressing the symptoms of poverty, while trying to preserve the life-giving aspects of informal settlements.

10 Jacobs, Jane. *The Death and Life of Great American Cities: The Failure of Town Planning*, (Victoria, Australia, Pelican Books, 1964), 25.

11 Alcorn, Randy. *Money Possessions and Eternity*, (Carol Stream, IL: Tyndale House Publishers. 2003), 354.

12   This situation only happens in communities that have been built for the poor. The poor who have built their homes and communities with their own sweat and blood will never intentionally destroy their own community and will fight to defend their neighborhoods from demolition.

13   *The Challenge of Slums*, 9.

14   Palen, John. *The Urban World* 7th ed., (New York, NY: McGraw-Hill, 2005), 242-3.

15   HACFM, *About Hope VI*, (The Housing Authority of the City of Fort Myers, 2018). Accessed June 21, 2018. http://www.hacfm.org/web/page.asp?urh=HopeVIInfo, para. 1-2.

16   These are also referred to as homeless camps. This is derogatory because it communicates that the residents still do not have a home. A tent or other semi-permanent structure might not meet middle-class building codes but it is still a home. To claim otherwise is a distortion of reality and an attack on the poor.

17   Newman, Bruce. *Inside San Jose's Largest Homeless Encampment, The Jungle*, (The Mercury News. August 12, 2016). Accessed February 21, 2018. https://www.mercurynews.com/2013/05/31/inside-san-joses-largest-homeless-encampment-the-jungle/, para. 5.

18   It must also be noted that over the years the residents have improved their homes. It is just a much slower process so as not to draw attention to the construction.

19   Gottdiener, Mark, and Leslie Budd. *Key Concepts in Urban Studies*, (London: SAGE Publications, 2005), 152.

20   Wheeler, Stephen M. *Planning for Sustainability: Creating Livable, Equitable, and Ecological Communities,* (New York, NY: Routledge, 2004), 66.

21   Ibid., 4.

22   Wilkinson, Richard, and Kate Pickett. *The Spirit Level: Why Greater Equality Makes Societies Stronger*, (New York, NY: Bloomsbury Press, 2010), 174.

23   Benesh, *Blueprints for a Just* City, 14.

24   *The Challenge of Slums*, 103.

25   Perkins, John. *Beyond Charity: The Call To Christian Community Development*, (Grand Rapids MI: Baker Books, 1993), 32.

26   Montgomery, Charles. *Happy City: Transforming Our Lives Through Urban Design*, (New York, NY: Farrar, Straus and Giroux, 2013), 60.

27   Gallagher, Leigh. *The End of the Suburbs: Where the American Dream is Moving*, (New York, NY: Portfolio/Penguin, 2013), 90.

28   Gottdiener and Budd, *Key Concepts in Urban Studies*, 94.

29   Korten, David. *When Corporations Rule the World*, 2nd Ed. (Bloomfield, CT: Kumarian Press, 2001), 84.

30   Palen, *The Urban World* 7th ed., 246.

31   Speck, Jeff. *Walkable City: How Downtown Can Save America, One Step at a Time*, (New York: Farrar, Straus and Giroux, 2012), 68.

32   Montgomery, *Happy City*, 243.

33   Gottdiener and Budd, *Key Concepts in Urban Studies*, 145.

34   Ibid., 112.

35   *Code of Hammurabi*, (Wright.edu), Accessed January 22, 2019. http://www.wright.edu/~christopher.oldstone-moore/Hamm.htm, para. 229, 233.

36   Deuteronomy 22:8 (NLT).

37   Garau, Pietro, Elliott D. Sclar, and Gabriella Y. Caroline. *A Home in the City: UN Millennium Project Task Force on Improving the Lives of Slum Dwellers*, (Sterling, VA: Earthscan, 2005), 63.

38   Montgomery, *Happy City*, 293.

39   Ibid., 65.

40   Speck, *Walkable City*, 105-106.

41   McKenna Associates Inc. *Zoning Ordinance: City of Rockwood, Michigan*, (Northville MI: 2008), Accessed June, 8, 2018. http://rockwoodmi.org/uploads/Library/Files/5-Building%20and%20Safety/Zoning/Rockwood%20Zoning%20Ordinance%20110308.pdf, 1-2.

42   Ibid., 3-3.

43   Garau, *A Home in the City*, 63.

44   Montgomery, *Happy City*, 66.

45   Jacobs, *The Death and Life of Great American Cities*, 20.

46   Palen, *The Urban World* 7th ed., 284.

47   This is based on 50 Philippine Pesos to 1 US Dollar exchange rate.

48   This is an individual living alone. He also receives regular assistance from a relative so his actual disposable income is slightly higher.

[49] Jacobs, *The Death and Life of Great American Cities*, 200.

[50] Weber, Max. *The City*. Translated and edited by Don Martindale and Gertrud Neuwirth, (New York, NY: Collier Books, 1962), 72-73.

[51] Gottdiener and Budd, *Key Concepts in Urban Studies*, 137-138.

[52] Adem, Elisea. *Urban Poverty: The Case of the Railway Squatters*, (Manila, Philippines: UST Press, 1992), 51.

[53] *The Challenge of Slums*, 100.

[54] Pieterse, Edgar. *City Futures: Confronting the Crisis of Urban Development*, (New York, NY: Zed Books, 2008), 57-58.

[55] Wheeler, *Planning for Sustainability*, 190.

[56] Adem, *Urban Poverty*, 62.

[57] De Soto, Hernando. *The Other Path: The Economic Answer to Terrorism*, (New York, NY: Basic Books, 1989), 243.

[58] Benesh, *Blueprints for a Just City*, 56.

[59] Jacobs, *The Death and Life of Great American Cities*, 105.

[60] A tricycle is a motorcycle with a sidecar used for transporting passengers.

[61] Jacobs, *The Death and Life of Great American Cities*, 217.

[62] Roseland, Mark. *Toward Sustainable Communities: Resources for Citizens and their Communities*. Revised Edition, (Gabriola Island, Canada: New Society Publishers, 2005), 135.

[63] Evans, Peter. Editor. *Livable Cities: Urban Struggle for Livelihood and Sustainability*, (Los Angeles, CA: University of California Press, 2002), 1.

[64] White, Randy. *Encounter God in the City: Onramps to Personal and Community Transformation*, (Downers Grove, IL: InterVarsity Press, 2006), 88.

[65] Nazal, Roberto. *Call to Action*. In *Sambahaginan: An Experience in Community Development Work*, (Quezon City: Institute for Studies in Asian Church and Culture, 1992), 66.

[66] Speck, *Walkable City*, 11.

[67] Gottdiener and Budd, *Key Concepts in Urban Studies*, 109.

[68] A jeepney is the main form of public transportation in the Philippines. They are modeled after World War II US troop transport vehicles and can hold about 20 passengers.

69   Every once in a while a car will attempt to enter Botocan, but because of all the pedestrians they are forced to drive at walking speed.

70   Jacobs, *The Death and Life of Great American Cities*, 239.

71   Montgomery, *Happy City*, 183.

72   Speck, *Walkable City*, 38.

73   Jacobs, *The Death and Life of Great American Cities*, 44.

74   A great activity on a free afternoon is to experience the difference between driving and walking a neighborhood. First, drive the streets particularly focusing on your emotions and how you perceive the community. Next, walk a few blocks observing the details of the neighborhood. Afterward, reflect on how your emotions and perception of the community changed when you parked your car and walked the streets.

75   Montgomery, Charles. *The Mayor Who Wowed the World Urban Forum: Bogota's Enrique Penalosa's Happy 'war on cars.'* (The Tyee, June 23, 2006), Accessed March 20, 2018. https://thetyee.ca/Views/2006/06/23/Mayor/, para. 6.

76   Dickenson, John, Bill Gould, Colin Clarke, Sandra Mather, Mansell Prothero, David Siddle, Clifford Smith and Elizabeth Thomas-Hope. *Geography of the Third World*, 2nd Ed. (New York: Routledge 1996), 214.

77   Allen still chooses to live in Botocan even though he can afford to move out.

78   Montgomery, *Happy City*, 55.

79   Korten, *When Corporations Rule the World*, 51.

80   Nouwen, Henri J.M. *Reaching Out: The Three Movements of the Spiritual Life*, (New York, NY: Doubleday, 1975), 25.

81   Jocano, F. Landa. *Slum as a Way of Life: A Study of Coping Behavior in an Urban Environment*, (Quezon City, Philippines: New Day Publishers, 1975), 172.

82   Ibid., 175.

83   Zechariah 8:4-5 (NLT).

84   In case you are wondering, yes, she still lives in Botocan.

85   This is not to say that everyone has to live like this. High-density walkable, mixed-use, mixed-income communities are certainly not appealing for everyone.

[86] Jacobs, *The Death and Life of Great American Cities*, 129.

[87] Gottdiener and Budd, *Key Concepts in Urban Studies*, 111.

[88] The figure of 6 people per acre is based on the population density of Manassas, VA, which has a population density of 4,201 people per square mile or about 6.5 people per acre. (Manassas, Virginia, Sperling's Best Places, Accessed April 2, 2019), https://www.bestplaces.net/people/city/virginia/manassas, para. 1.

[89] Gallagher, *The End of the Suburbs*, 60.

[90] Camuti, Liz. *Sprawl Costs the U.S. $1 Trillion Annually*, (The Dirt, September 22, 2015), Accessed January 10, 2017 https://dirt.asla.org/2015/09/22/sprawl-costs-the-u-s-1-trillion-annually/, para. 1.

[91] Montgomery, *Happy City*, 260.

[92] Neuwirth, *Shadow Cities*, 301.

[93] Of course, you cannot just say you care more about your property value than the suffering of others, so the phrase "quality of life" is often substituted for property value. The argument goes something like, "Having homeless people living in tiny homes next door will lower my quality of life."

[94] Jacobs, *The Death and Life of Great American Cities*, 242.

[95] Schwartz, Samuel. *Street Smart: The Rise of Cities and the Fall of Cars*, (New York, NY: Public Affairs, 2015), 109.

[96] Speck, *Walkable City*, 82.

[97] Summers, Nick. *New York City Embraces a Bold New Traffic Theory*, (Newsweek, February 26, 2009). Accessed April 2, 2018. http://www.newsweek.com/new-york-city-embraces-bold-new-traffic-theory-82647, para. 4.

[98] Schwartz, *Street Smart*, 109-110.

[99] Speck, *Walkable City*, 148.

[100] Without extra rooms for storage, the roof is a convenient place to keep recyclables to be sold.

[101] The lack of sewage is one of the areas where the city government has failed the residents.

[102] Evans, *Livable Cities*, 16.

[103] Glaeser, Edward. *If You Love Nature, Move to the City*, (The Boston Globe, February 10, 2011), Accessed April 2, 2018.

104 http://archive.boston.com/bostonglobe/editorial_opinion/oped/article
s/2011/02/10/if_you_love_nature_move_to_the_city/, para. 3.

104 Speck, *Walkable City*, 52.

105 Rybczynski, Witold. *Makeshift Metropolis: Ideas About Cities*,
(New York, NY: Scribner, 2010), 188-189.

106 Garau, *A Home in the City*, 3.

107 Ibid., 3.

108 Chambers, Edward. *Roots for Radicals: Organizing for Power,
Action, and Justice*, (New York, NY: Continuum International
Publishing, 2004), 13.

109 *The Challenge of Slums*, 5.

110 Wilkinson and Pickett, *The Spirit Level*, 29.

111 Ibid., 181.

112 Garau, *A Home in the City*, 62.

113 Global Health Observatory Data. *Number of Road Traffic Deaths*,
(World Health Organization, 2018), Accessed June 8, 2018.
http://www.who.int/gho/road_safety/mortality/traffic_deaths_numbe
r/en/, para. 1.

114 LeBeau, Phil, Editor. *Traffic Deaths Edge Lower, but 2017 Stats
Paint Worrisome Picture*, (CNBC, February 15, 2018), Accessed
June 8, 2018. https://www.cnbc.com/2018/02/14/traffic-deaths-
edge-lower-but-2017-stats-paint-worrisome-picture.html. para. 2.

115 Marohn, Charles. *Confessions of a Recovering Engineer*, (Strong
Towns, November 22, 2010), Accessed May 7, 2018.
https://www.strongtowns.org/journal/2010/11/22/confessions-of-a-
recovering-engineer.html. para. 10.

116 Ibid., para. 1.

117 Revising zoning laws does not mean using different terminology
such as in parts of Texas. Instead of zoning, Texas has homeowners
associations and laws protecting property value that essentially
function as traditional zoning laws; creating sprawl and protecting
property values at the expense of the poor.

118 Wheeler, *Planning for Sustainability*, 155.

119 Jacobsen, Eric O. *Sidewalks in the Kingdom: New Urbanism and the
Christian Faith*, (Grand Rapids, MI: Brazos Press, 2003), 88.

120 Jacobs, *The Death and Life of Great American Cities*, 187.

121 Garau, *A Home in the City*, 63.

[122] By mixed-use, I do not mean a corner store owned by a non-resident, but truly mixed-use by allowing households to operate small businesses from their home. This also assumes that the other positive features of informal settlements have also been adopted.

[123] Wheeler, *Planning for Sustainability*, 61.

[124] O'Rourke, Dara. *Community-Driven Regulation: Towards an Improved Model of Environmental Regulation in Vietnam.* In *Livable Cities: Urban Struggle for Livelihood and Sustainability*, (Los Angeles, CA: University of California Press, 2002), 99-100.

[125] Greenfield, Craig. *Subversive Jesus: An Adventure in Justice, Mercy, and Faithfulness in a Broken World*, (Grand Rapids MI: Zondervan, 2016), 35.

[126] Montgomery, *Happy City*, 128.

[127] Jacobs, *The Death and Life of Great American Cities*, 285.

[128] Ibid., 33.

[129] Schwartz, *Street Smart*, 216.

[130] Speck, *Walkable City*, 69.

[131] Garau, *A Home in the City*, 62.

[132] Duenas, Alejandra. *First 'No Car Day' of 2017 in Bogota Gets Underway*, (The City Paper, February 2, 2017), Accessed February 26, 2018. https://thecitypaperbogota.com/bogota/first-no-car-day-in-bogota-gets-underway/16050, para. 1.

[133] Roseland, *Toward Sustainable Communities*, 119.

[134] Jacobs, *The Death and Life of Great American Cities*, 233.

[135] Rybczynski, *Makeshift Metropolis*, 146.

[136] Tzu, Lao. (Goodreads), Accessed April 22, 2019. https://www.goodreads.com/quotes/215411-go-to-the-people-live-with-them-learn-from-them, para. 1.

[137] Korten, *When Corporations Rule the World*, 116.

[138] Greenfield, *Subversive Jesus*, 107.

[139] Gallagher, *The End of the Suburbs*, 62.

[140] Montgomery, *Happy City*, 250.

[141] Neuwirth, *Shadow Cities*, 302.

[142] Palen, *The Urban World* 7th ed., 239.

[143] Jacobs, *The Death and Life of Great American Cities*, 122.

[144] Ibid., 284.

[145] This understanding of self-deception is adopted from *Leadership and Self-Deception: Getting Out of the Box*, 2nd Ed. The Arbinger Institute, (San Francisco, CA: Berrett-Koehler Publishers, 2010).

[146] Newman, *Inside San Jose's Largest Homeless Encampment, The Jungle*, para. 6.

[147] Blake, Evan. *San Jose, California: "The Jungle" homeless camp dismantled*, (World Socialists Web Site, December, 2014), Accessed by author February 15, 2019. https://www.wsws.org/en/articles/2014/12/09/home-d09.html, para. 6-7.

[148] Ibid., para. 7.

[149] Ibid., para. 8.

[150] Ibid., para. 3.

[151] *The Challenge of Slums*, 127.

[152] Gottdiener and Budd, *Key Concepts in Urban Studies*, 80.

[153] Kramer, Mark. *Dispossessed: Life in Our World's Urban Slums*, (Maryknoll, NY: Orbis Books, 2005), 34-35.

[154] De Soto, *The Other Path*, 244.

[155] Pieterse, *City Futures*, 57.

[156] Neuwirth, *Shadow Cities*, 302.

[157] Ibid., 301.

[158] Garau, *A Home in the City*, 89.

[159] Perkins, *Beyond Charity*, 120.

[160] *The Challenge of Slums*, 74.

[161] This is usually called *slum upgrading*, but I am intentionally avoiding that term because the common use of *slum upgrading* is different from what I am presenting.

[162] See chapter 12 for a detailed discussion on living where you serve.

[163] Home-based businesses in walkable, mixed-use communities do not need to provide parking for customers because their customers walk. Likewise, they do not cause extra traffic.

[164] Garau, *A Home in the City*, 89.

[165] Jacobs, *The Death and Life of Great American Cities*, 247.